". . . we have aimed to please those who prefer simple reading, as well as to make it easy for the studious who wish to commit things to memory, and to be helpful to all."

(2 Maccabees 2:25)

FIFTY FUNERAL HOMILIES

by

REV. MSGR. CHAS. HUGO DOYLE

Christian Classics, Inc.
Westminster, Maryland 21157
1984

First published, 1984

NIHIL OBSTAT: MSGR. CARROLL E. SATTERFIELD
CENSOR LIBRORUM

IMPRIMATUR: MOST REV. WILLIAM D. BORDERS, D. D.
ARCHBISHOP OF BALTIMORE

FEBRUARY 3, 1984

FIFTY FUNERAL HOMILIES

ACKNOWLEDGMENTS

The author acknowledges with gratitude the gracious permissions granted by the following publishers to quote from their works protected by copyright:

—*ILLUSTRATIONS FROM ART*, by James Burns, M.A., published by James Clarke and Company, Ltd., Cambridge, England. 1912. Introductory material for Seventh Homily taken from page 305; for the Twenty-second Homily from page 321; for the Twenty-fourth Homily from page 307; for the Twenty-fifth Homily from page 320; for the Twenty-eighth Homily from page 320.

—*THE TREASURY OF SERMON ILLUSTRATIONS*, edited by Charles L. Wallis, copyright 1950, by Pierce & Smith. Used to introduce the Tenth Homily, with Abingdon's permission.

—*THE SPEAKER'S BOOK OF ILLUSTRATIVE STORIES*, edited by Maxwell Drake, Drake House, Indianapolis, Ind., 1956. Story on page 81 is used to introduce the Twenth-sixth Homily.

—*1001 ILLUSTRATIONS FOR PULPIT AND PLATFORM*, by Aquilla Webb, published by Harper and Row Publishers, Inc., N.Y. 1926. Introduction to the Thirty-ninth Homily from page 188.

—*THE DOCUMENTS OF VATICAN II*, edited by Rev. Walter M. Abbott, S. J., excerpts from page 215—The Mystery of Death, reprinted with the permission of America Press, Inc., 106 W. 56th. Street, New York, N.Y., 10019. © 1966. All Rights Reserved.

—The Holy Scripture texts used in this work are taken from *THE NEW AMERICAN BIBLE*, copyright © 1970, by The Confraternity of Christian Doctrine, Washington, D.C., and used with permission. All Rights Reserved.

All royalties from the sale of *FIFTY FUNERAL HOMILIES* have been assigned to the *NAZARETH LIFE CENTER*, P.O. Box 242, Garrison, New York, 10524. The Center has been founded and is directed by Father Eugene Keane, as a haven for unmarried mothers who have chosen life as an alternative to abortion. The Center is staffed by devoted Franciscan Missionary Sisters of the Sacred Heart of Peekskill, N.Y.

The author considers the work of the Nazareth Life Center as a most worthy work of charity since it does not receive or accept State or Federal funding. Gifts are tax deductible.

CONTENTS

Preface
Numbered Homilies

1. General 2
2. General 4
3. General 6
4. General 8
5. For a person brought home
   for burial in family plot 10
6. General 12
7. General 14
8. Funeral with sad
   circumstances 16
9. General 18
10. General 20
11. For a charitable widow........ 22
12. General 24
13. General 26
14. For a young girl 28
15. General 30
16. For a charitable woman 32
17. General 34
18. General 36
19. General 38
20. General 40
21. General 42
22. General 44
23. General 46
24. For a young person 48
25. General 50

26. General 52
27. General 54
28. General 56
29. For an infant-young child 58
30. General 60
31. General 62
32. General 64
33. General 66
34. General 68
35. General 70
36. General 72
37. General 74
38. General 76
39. General 78
40. General 80
41. General 82
42. General 84
43. General 86
44. For an exemplary
    person 88
45. General 90
46. Loss of son or daughter 92
47. General 94
48. Death with tragic
    circumstances 96
49. General 98
50. General 100

PREFACE

Throughout my priesthood of over fifty years, the preparation of homilies for funeral Masses has always been a burden. The element of time, usually two days, militates against thoughtful and adequate preparation. A solution, of course, would be to have a series of homilies prepared in advance. The day for one or two homilies for use at funerals is past. Not infrequently, people who attend daily Mass take advantage of a later Mass, such as a funeral. Another reason might be given for the same persons being at funeral Masses: in smaller communities, a death in a family touches the whole neighborhood, parish, or community, and so it is that the same people attend many funerals. Obviously, for the reasons cited, the celebrant cannot get by with only one or two homilies. He must have a sizable portfolio of funeral homilies, and he must constantly be on the lookout for new material.

Prior to my retirement, I resolved to do my best to write a series of homilies for use at funeral Masses in the hope that such a collection might spare some busy priests precious time and effort. This collection may well afford homilists some seed thoughts around which they might develop their own presentation, or draw from the introduction or theme, their own ingenious applications.

In the writing of these homilies, I was guided somewhat by a *Letter to the Editor* I read in a Catholic newspaper. It was from a lady who had attended a funeral Mass for a relative. The writer was shaken by the insensitivity of the homilist to the distress and sorrow of the family, and by the rambling presentation of his theme.

It is my personal feeling that the aim of every funeral homily should be twofold: to instruct and comfort. While perhaps it is too much to hope that the immediate family of the deceased will be capable of assimilating much instruction, nevertheless, they will be conscious of the homilist's least effort to sympathize with them; and they will be grateful. The rest of the congregation will be more amenable to instructions on the mystery of life and death, the goodness and mercy of God, the resurrection of the body.

It is respectfully suggested that the homilist jot down on the margins of the pages the date of the use of the illustrative introductions. This will guard against too frequent use of the same material.

FIRST HOMILY

General

Extension of sympathy to the family

Introduction

On behalf of the priests of the parish, the trustees, the parish council and the parishioners, I extend deep sympathy to the family and relatives of _____.

My dear friends, if there is ever a time when one needs a deep and abiding faith, it is on the occasion of the funeral of a loved one. There is such a stark sense of finality about death that it is easy to drift into a hopeless attitude and begin to think that death is the end of everything.

To offset this, the Church, in the Liturgy of the Word, draws on readings from Holy Scripture to confirm our faith that death is not the end; rather, it is the doorway to another and better life in the kingdom of heaven. In the Eucharistic Prayer leading to the consecration in the Mass for the dead, we read these stirring words:

> In him who rose from the dead, our hope of resurrection dawned. The sadness of death gives way to the bright promise of immortality. Lord, for your faithful people, life is changed, not ended. When the body of our earthly dwelling lies in death, we gain an everlasting dwelling place in heaven.

In the words of that prayer we have a summary of the Church's doctrine concerning death and life after death.

Application

Let us consider the time our Lord made a two-day journey on foot to a cemetery to visit the grave of His friend Lazarus, whom He loved, and to console Martha and Mary, the dead man's sisters. The sisters had managed to get word to our Lord that their brother was gravely ill, but He deliberately waited two days before setting out for Bethany, saying to His disciples: "Our beloved Lazarus has fallen asleep, and I am going there to wake him."

Hearing that Christ was nearing the village, Martha went to meet Him and said: "Lord, if you had been here, my brother would never have died. Even now, I am sure that God will give you whatever you ask of him." Jesus assured her: "Your brother will rise again." Martha replied, "I know he will rise again in the resurrection on the last day." Jesus told her, "I am the resurrection and the life: whoever believes in me will come to life; and whoever is alive and believes in me will never die. Do you believe this?" "Yes, Lord," she replied. "I have come to believe that you are the Messiah, the Son of God: he who is to come into the world" (Jn. 11:21–27).

Note well how our Lord exacted an act of faith on the part of Martha before actually arriving at the tomb of Lazarus. Once there, giving free vent to His feelings, "He wept." Composing Himself, our Lord ordered the stone to be removed from the front of the tomb, at which time Martha reminded Him that her brother had been in the tomb for four days. That remark prompted Christ to exact from Martha a renewal of her act of faith, saying: "Did I not assure you that if you believed you would see the glory of God displayed?"

It was then and only then that Christ called Lazarus to come forth from the tomb, bound hand and foot with linen strips, his face wrapped in a cloth. "Untie him," Jesus told them, "and let him go free" (Jn. 11:44).

The raising of Lazarus from the dead had its designed effect. It caused many of the Jews who had come to visit Mary, and had seen what Jesus had done, to put their faith in Him. After the stone was removed from the front of the tomb, Christ raised His eyes upward and said: "Father, I thank you for having heard me. I know that you always hear me, but I have said this for the sake of the crowd, that they may believe that you sent me."

Conclusion

Just as Christ demanded an act of faith from Martha, He likewise demands an act of faith from each one of us here today. In the presence of death, Christ wants us to show Him that we really believe what we have said in our morning and evening prayers when they included the Apostles' Creed. Then, it seemed so easy to say: "I believe in the resurrection of the body and life everlasting." At every Sunday Mass, we have said in the Profession of Faith: "We look for the resurrection of the dead and the life of the world to come." Perhaps those words have been glossed over by us in the past, but this very day they have a new reality; and we must give them full assent.

After the consecration at this Mass, the same Christ who stood at the tomb of His beloved friend Lazarus will be present on this altar. He who wept with Martha and Mary over the death of their brother will understand our grief and tears, and will say to each of us, "_____
_____ will rise again on the last day; do you believe this?" With every bit of faith we can muster, let us reply, "Yes, Lord, I believe, for you have the words of eternal life."

Our earnest hope is that the soul of _____ has already heard those comforting and triumphant words: "This day you will be with me in paradise" (Lk. 23:43). The mortal body we honor today will rise in its perfection from the grave on the last day—to be reunited with his (her) soul to enjoy the bliss of eternal happiness with God in heaven. Amen.

SECOND HOMILY

General

Extension of sympathy to the family

Introduction

One day some translators of the Old Testament were working on the Book of Malachi. When they came upon verse three in chapter three, they were puzzled by the wording: God was not pleased with the quality of the service rendered at that time by some of the Old Testament priests. He promised to send the Messenger of the Covenant to reform them, saying: "He will sit refining and purifying (silver), and he will purify the sons of Levi, refining them like gold or like silver that they may offer due sacrifice to the LORD" (Mal. 3:3).

The translators wondered whether the word *sit* had any special significance; after some discussion, they decided to ask a noted silversmith for his opinion. At a meeting with the group, the old silversmith was asked why it was necessary to *sit* during the refining process of precious metals. He told them that an expert silversmith would sit by the refiner's fire and watch the gold or silver being separated from the dross; and when he was able to see the clear reflection of his face in the molten gold or silver, then, and only then, was the precious metal poured off into ingots.

Application

I have often thought that, during the long illness of _____ _____, the Divine Silversmith sat by his (her) bedside supporting him (her) in the most agonizing sufferings, and revealing to him (her) the deep meaning of the inspired words of St. Peter, who said of suffering: "There is cause for rejoicing here. You may for a time have to suffer the distress of many trials; but this is so that your faith, which is more precious than the passing splendor of fire-tried gold, may by its genuineness lead to praise, glory, and honor when Jesus Christ appears" (1 Pet. 1:6–7). Indeed, I am convinced that our Lord was nearer to _____ during his (her) terminal sufferings than perhaps at any other time in his (her) whole life; and when Christ's bruised, buffeted, thorn-crowned face was perfectly reflected in the soul of _____, the Savior took him (her) to Himself.

Suffering is one of the great mysteries of life. The author of *The Imitation of Christ* writes: "If anything had been better and more beneficial for man's salvation than suffering, Christ would have shown it by word and example." We call ourselves Christians, and a Christian is a follower of Christ. Willingness to suffer with Christ equips the Christian with the power to conquer sin. St. Peter reminds us of this in these words: "Christ suffered in the flesh; therefore arm yourselves with the same mentality" (1 Pet. 4:1).

St. Peter, the first Vicar of Christ on earth, saw in suffering a purgation and cleansing as when gold or silver is purified by the smelting process, for he wrote: "Do not be surprised, beloved, that a trial by fire is occurring in your midst. It is a test for you, but it should not catch you off guard. Rejoice, instead, in the measure that you share Christ's sufferings. When his glory is revealed, you will rejoice exultantly" (1 Pet. 4:12–13).

St. Luke in his Gospel notes that our Lord had two disciples who became disillusioned and discouraged over His cruel death and subsequent burial. They had earnestly hoped that He was the promised Messiah; but there it was, three days after the crucifixion and burial, and there were only rumors that He had risen as He said He would; so they started home to Emmaus. As they walked along, they discussed the happenings of the last three days and they were dejected. A stranger, as they thought, caught up with them and asked what they were discussing and why they were so sad.

The two disciples were amazed that there was anyone who had not heard about what had happened in Jerusalem those last three days; they recounted in detail what had happened to Jesus. When they finished, our Lord said to them: "What little sense you have! How slow you are to believe all that the prophets have announced! Did not the Messiah have to undergo all this so as to enter into his glory?" (Lk. 24:25–26)

Conclusion

Ask me why _____ had to suffer so much and for so long, and my only answer is that it was God's will and plan for him (her) before entering into his (her) glory. If he (she) could speak to us this morning, he (she) would repeat the words of St. Paul: "I consider the sufferings of the present to be as nothing compared with the glory to be revealed in us" (Rom. 8:18).

May the family find comfort in these words of the blind Milton: "Death is the golden key that opens the palace of eternity."

May you, good and faithful servant, enter into the joy of your Lord for an eternity of happiness.

THIRD HOMILY

General

Extension of sympathy to the family

Introduction

Dearly beloved, when Queen Elizabeth I of England was on her deathbed, she went into a panic at the thought of dying. There she was, with five thousand gowns in her wardrobe and an empire at her feet, yet she tossed from side to side, crying out: "Any amount for a little more time."

Now come with me to another deathbed, that of St. Therese of the Child Jesus, better known as the Little Flower of Jesus. We find her in her cold, dark monastery cell. The tuberculosis had wrought its havoc, and the end was approaching. When this twenty-four-year-old religious felt the onslaught of the final hemorrhage, she did not light her lamp for fear someone would come to her help, and somehow, delay her union with God in heaven. Here we have the two extremes; an awful and exaggerated fear of death, and an irrepressible longing to be united with God.

Application

Christ, the Son of God, assumed our human nature; and He knows through that same human nature how man fears death. Indeed, on the very eve of His Passion, did He not sweat blood and cry out to His Heavenly Father: "Abba (O Father), you have the power to do all things. Take this cup away from me. But let it be as you would have it, not as I" (Mk. 14:36). These striking words of our Redeemer tell us how each of us must face death and the sufferings leading to it. We must see in death the will of God and submit to it.

St. Paul tells us that our Lord died to ransom us from our sins and the fear of death. Hear him say:

> Now, since the children are men of blood and flesh, Jesus likewise had a full share in ours, that by his death he might rob the devil, the prince of death, of his power, and free those who through fear of death had been slaves their whole life long (Heb. 2:14–15).

There is no doubt that Christ conquered death by His own death on the cross; and, as a consequence, we should have no exaggerated fear of it. Did Christ not say: "I am the resurrection and the life: whoever believes in me, though he should die, will come to life; and whoever is alive and believes in me will never die" (Jn. 11:26)? In His own death, Christ set a pattern for all of us to follow. For instance, His last words on the cross were, "Father, into your hands I commend my spirit" (Lk.

23:46), showing, thereby, that as His followers all Christians must make the final surrender of their soul to God.

St. Stephen, the first Christian martyr, followed Christ's example in the face of death. Holy Scripture tells us that during the moving speech before the council, St. Stephen "looked to the sky above and saw the glory of God, and Jesus standing at God's right hand." When he related what he saw to the council, he was rushed and dragged outside the city; and the stoning began. St. Stephen was heard to say: "Lord Jesus, receive my spirit"; and then he died (Acts 7:59). _____

_____ suffered through a long and painful illness, and he (she) was a model of patience and resignation. Who could say for sure that he (she), during the long sleepless nights, had not, like St. Stephen, seen the gentle Christ standing in glory at the right hand of His Father? Be that as it may, he (she) surrendered his (her) purified soul to God, and in peace fell asleep in the Lord.

Conclusion

Tragedy would compound sorrow if this Christian funeral was little more than a vehicle for venting our emotions of love or grief. In all truth, a funeral should provoke the virtues of faith and hope in each one of us. It should project us into the future to the time when we must submit ourselves to the will of God as to the time, place, and circumstances of our own death. Each of us must live every day as if it were our last day on earth. Let us resolve to be submissive to God's will in the trials and tribulations He permits or sends us. Job was chastised in a frightful manner, physically and, even more, spiritually. His wife mocked him for his submission to God's will: "Curse God and die," she said to her husband. Job's reply was: "We accept good things from God; and should we not accept evil?" (Job 2:9–10)

St. Rose of Lima (1586–1617) tells of a private revelation to her from our Lord wherein He said of pain, sufferings, and trials:

> Let all men know that grace comes after affliction. Let them know that without the burden of afflictions it is impossible to reach the height of grace . . . This is the only true stairway to paradise, and without the cross, they can find no road to climb to heaven.

God the Father did not spare His only Son from death on the cross. Suffering and death were the coins of mankind's ransom. Christ did not spare His Mother Mary from witnessing His redemptive sacrifice. She brought Him into the world, and she would watch over His death. Christ's death was the sharpest sword that opened her heart, but thereby she assumed a new role of mothering mankind in life and in death.

O Mary, Mother of Sorrows, succor us now in this hour of need!

FOURTH HOMILY

General

Extension of sympathy to the family

Introduction

My dear friends, it is related that King Louis XIV of France, shortly after his ascent to the throne, stood at an open window of his study in the palace, silently admiring the simple beauty of the Church of St. Denis standing some distance away. A servant ventured to remark that all the monarch's ancestors lay buried in that church, and that, doubtless, it would be the new king's last resting place. The very next day the king ordered plans drawn for a wing to be built so that he wouldn't have to see that church every time he looked out that particular window.

Application

Many people are like that. The thought of death depresses them. The Council Fathers of Vatican II were much more practical. They faced the problem of death head-on, saying:

> It is in the face of death that the riddle of human existence becomes most acute. Not only is man tormented by pain and by the advancing deterioration of his body, but even more so by the dread of perpetual extinction. He rightly follows the intuition of his heart when he abhors and repudiates the absolute ruin and total disappearance of his own person . . . Although the mystery of death utterly beggars the imagination, the Church has been taught by divine revelation, and herself firmly teaches, that man has been created by God for a blissful purpose beyond the reach of earthly misery.

I am sure the members of the family of _____ agree with the Council Fathers that "the mystery of death beggars the imagination." Numbed by the suddenness of the passing away, distraught by the loss of a loved one, preoccupied with all the various minute details of the funeral arrangements, and the sad social duty of meeting friends to receive their condolences: all this has left little time to consider what has really happened. And now we are gathered in this church to join in the offering of the Holy Sacrifice of the Mass. Indeed, in this Mass, the very Son of God, Jesus Christ Himself, becomes a Victim to be offered to His Father for the repose of the soul of _____ _____. It is consoling to think that the Victim who pleads for the deceased in this Mass, Himself suffered death and was raised from the dead.

There is no doubt that the family will be fortified by this Mass for the ordeal to follow, that of the committal of the hallowed body of the deceased to the earth in the cemetery, and the sad journey home. This could well be the saddest day of your life, but, through your tears, make every effort to remember that his (her) soul, being in its nature spiritual, is therefore immortal; and there is no interruption in the life of the soul. The Sacred Congregation for the Doctrine of the Faith, in a letter dated May 17, 1979, confirmed the constant teaching of the Church that the human soul is a "spiritual element endowed with consciousness and will, and survives after death, so that the 'human self' subsists."

Have you ever had relatives or close friends who, for whatever reason, decide to return to the country of their birth, there to live out their remaining years? The thought of such a separation depresses you. When the day comes for the departure, you accompany them to the airport. Tears may come to your eyes as you bid them farewell. You watch the plane take off, and you keep looking until the plane is lost to view in the clouds. Certainly, the departure is painful, but somehow you are consoled by the thought of the joy they will experience upon landing on their native soil, and being welcomed by relatives and friends eagerly awaiting their arrival.

Conclusion

Surely, it is a sad task for us today to have to say goodbye to the mortal remains of _____, but let us think of the spiritual joy of his (her) immortal soul at seeing God, at being in the presence of the Blessed Virgin Mary and the angels and saints. Not the least of the joys will be the welcome from relatives and friends who have gone on before him (her).

At the end of the world, God will call from the grave the body we honor here today. It will rise in all its perfection, and soul and body will be together in eternal bliss in heaven with God.

Henry Cardinal Newman penned these lines before he died. I quote them here because they seem to reflect the prayer of _____ _____.

Lead, Savior, lead me home in childlike faith,
   Home to my God,
To rest forever after earthly strife,
In the calm light of everlasting life.

Eternal rest grant unto him (her), O Lord, and let perpetual light shine upon him (her). Amen.

FIFTH HOMILY

For a person brought home for burial in the family plot

Extension of sympathy to the family

Introduction

Sarah, wife of Abraham, died in the city of Kiriath-arba (that is, Hebron) in the land of Canaan, at the age of one hundred and twenty-seven years. Abraham, Scripture tells us, performed the customary mourning rites for his wife, and then stepped aside and addressed the Hittites in these words: "Although I am a resident alien among you, sell me from your holdings a piece of property for a burial ground, that I may bury my dead wife" (Gen. 23:4).

The Hittites offered Abraham the use of the finest of their sepulchers in which to bury Sarah, and the Patriarch bowed low to them in gratitude, yet asked that Ephron, the Hittite, sell him a piece of property that had two caves on it. Ephron offered the land as a gift, but Abraham would not hear of it. He paid Ephron four hundred shekels of silver for the land and thus the field with the two caves was transferred from the Hittites to Abraham as a burial place for Sarah, himself, and his descendants.

Abraham wanted a permanent burial site as a personal possession, a place made sure, a sacred spot facing Hebron in the land of Canaan. Sarah was buried in the cave of the field of Machpelah. Abraham was himself buried in that family plot, as was Isaac and his wife Rebekah; and Leah also rests there. Jacob, too, was buried in that hallowed resting place (Gen. 49:31–33).

Application

It would appear that it is inherent in us to derive comfort and solace from the thought of family members being together even in death. Abraham felt that way, and so did the parents of a nineteen-year-old son killed in action. Pfc. Joseph Hartley was killed some forty years ago on a German battlefield. The young soldier disappeared in a spray of enemy machine-gun fire as his company battled for a hill. He was buried where he fell.

A few months ago, a German farmer came upon the grave on his property by accident. He notified the authorities, and the body was identified as that of Pfc. Joseph Hartley and flown home to the United States for burial, with full military honors, in his native South Carolina. His elderly parents both attended the rites for their only child who gave his life for his country. They expressed their relief and gratitude for having their brave son home again.

Conclusion

The fact that the mortal remains of _____ have been returned to this village (town, city, community) for burial with the other members of his (her) family is evidence of the nearly universal belief that death does not break family ties, but rather strengthens them. Why this strong desire to be buried with close relatives who have pre-deceased him (her), if it does not indicate the strong belief that there is a spiritual fellowship among the dead of a family as well as between the dead and the living members? The reason may well be because love is indestructible!

Our holy religion teaches us that the dead are not lost to us; they have but passed into a higher, safer life, where they are secure from every trial and pain, and able to be advocates with God for us. If death were the absolute end of man's existence, this world would be nothing but a massive graveyard wherein a loving God allows to happen what man instinctively abhors and repudiates—absolute extinction. To do this, God would have to repudiate His promise of an eternity of bliss to those who know, love, and serve Him in this life.

In *The Credo of the People of God* by Pope Paul VI, these words afford comfort to those plunged into agony over the loss of a loved one. The saintly Pontiff wrote:

> "We believe that the multitude of those gathered around Jesus and Mary in Paradise forms the Church of Heaven, where they also, in different degrees, are associated with the holy Angels in the divine rule exercised by Christ in glory, interceding for us and helping our weakness by their brotherly care."

No, death is not the end, but the beginning of a new and better life with God. Let us show our abiding love for our dead by remembering them in our prayers, in the reception of Holy Communion, and in Masses offered and/or heard in suffrage for them. Do not hesitate to implore your deceased loved ones to intercede for you before the throne of God.

These lines from a memorial card sum it all up clearly:

Love is indestructible,
Its holy flame forever burneth;
From heaven it came, to heaven returneth.

_____, go in peace to love the Lord.

SIXTH HOMILY

General

Extension of sympathy to the family

Introduction

Many years ago I read a story of a little boy whose mother was gravely ill. A doctor was called; and after his examination, he wrote a prescription for a medicine that had to be secured promptly and immediately administered if the woman was to live. The young lad was told to take his bicycle and go as quickly as he could to the village pharmacy, have the prescription filled, and return as swiftly as he could. The road to the village took him past a thicket; and out of the corner of his eye he caught sight of an elusive type of butterfly, one for which he had been searching for a long time to add to his collection. How long he had spent trying to capture the rare butterfly he could not remember; however, by the time he got to the village, had the prescription filled, and returned home with the medicine, his mother had passed away.

Application

That story points up the fact that many of us act as the thoughtless little boy did. We forget the all-important reason for our existence in this world, and we become so enamored of the world, places, persons, and material things that we lose sight of the fact that we are but pilgrims on the road to heaven, our true home. So earth-bound are we that we resent having to leave this world, and death is considered a calamity, even an injustice.

The literary world is aghast at the number of books being published on death. Eight such books appeared recently at one time. The publisher of *On Death and Dying* has sold nearly a million copies. *The Denial of Death* was awarded the Pulitzer Prize for general non-fiction. There is no question but that death is a great mystery to millions of people, and they are searching for answers. Let it be said here that no one can understand death who does not understand the reason God created mankind and placed us on the earth He created for us.

Holy Scripture expressly declares that God has a purpose for everything He makes (Prov. 16:4); that purpose is clearly stated in these inspired words: "Everyone who is named as mine, whom I created for *my glory,* whom I formed and made" (Isa. 43:7). From this it is clear that the purpose of life here on earth is to give glory to God. The catechism tells us that God created us to *know, love,* and *serve* Him in this life and to be happy with Him in heaven in the next life. We *know* God through faith, the Scriptures, Tradition, and the teachings of the Church; we *love* God by keeping His commandments; and we *serve*

God through prayer, in fulfilling of the duties of our state in life, and in loving and serving our neighbor out of love for Him.

It was out of love for us that God created us. He wanted to share His happiness with us, but He willed that our life on earth be a testing period. We must prove ourselves worthy of eternal happiness with God. God *gives* heaven to no one—we must merit it in this life.

Death was not in the plans God had for our first parents and their descendants. Had Adam not sinned, we all would have been spared the agony we are going through today. Nowhere in the world would there have ever been a cemetery. But Adam did sin, and that sin called *original*, was so offensive to God that it closed heaven to all mankind; it flooded this world with woes, not the least of which is death. God loved fallen man so much that He sent His own Divine Son to become man to redeem us through His cruel death on the cross. Through Christ's death we were ransomed; heaven was opened to the just; and death was conquered. Christ's resurrection from the grave is an earnest of our resurrection from the grave on the last day, in physical perfection, to be united with our spiritual soul to live forever, in the bliss of heaven with God.

Conclusion

It is worthy of special note that the feasts of the saints were traditionally set to correspond to the day of their death, not to the day of their birth, with two notable exceptions: that of our Blessed Lady and of St. John the Baptist. We have every right to hope that the day of _____'s death was his (her) birthday into heaven's eternal joy with God.

At this funeral Mass, I hope your faith will somehow move you, in spite of your sorrow and tears, to say to him (her) in quiet prayer: "Happy Birthday!"

SEVENTH HOMILY

General

Extension of sympathy to the family

Introduction

My dear friends, one evening William Wordsworth and a friend were walking by the side of Loch Katrine at sunset. A lady was approaching them from the opposite direction, and in acknowledgment of the tipping of their hats to her, she asked: "Gentlemen, are you stepping westward?" The expression "stepping westward" stuck in Wordsworth's mind, and that night he wrote:

Stepping westward seem'd to be
A kind of heavenly destiny. . .
Its power was felt: and while my eye
Was fix'd upon the flowing sky,
A heavenly sweetness with the thought
Of travelling through the world that lay
Before me in my endless way.

Application

The first faltering unsteady steps of a tiny child are but the prelude to stepping westward into the sunset of life. The span of the intervening years may be short or long. The struggles and the sufferings are but strengthening and purifying forces, while the joys of life are but fore-tastes of eternal bliss. The Council Fathers of Vatican II assure us

that all mankind has been created by God for a blissful purpose beyond the reach of earthly misery . . . For God has called man and still calls him, so that with his entire being he might be joined to him in an endless sharing of a divine life beyond all corruption. Christ won the victory when he rose to life, since by his death he freed man from death.

Wordsworth's poem *Stepping Forward* aptly describes the life and the passing of _____. He (She) never lost sight of his (her) heavenly destiny. With admirable resignation he (she) faced the sunset of his (her) earthly life, with his (her) eyes "fix'd upon the flowing sky," and with a strong faith that aroused hope that he (she) would find eternal happiness with God.

Perhaps for those left to mourn him (her), it is most difficult to accept and give firm assent to the teaching of the Church that the life he (she) has entered into, far surpasses anything our poor earthbound minds can even imagine. Pope St. Gregory the Great laid the blame for this on Adam, saying that his sin caused man to lose sight of the joys of heaven. The saint explained it this way: while Adam was in the Garden of Eden,

God talked to him as a father to his son, and by purity of heart and heavenly vision, Adam was in a "paradise of pleasure" (Gen. 2:15).

After the fall, Adam lost that light of soul which, prior to his sin, he enjoyed abundantly. That sin caused him to be deprived of sanctifying grace, and caused heaven to be closed to him and his descendants: and all mankind would have to submit to death. Separated from God by his sin, banished from the Garden of Eden, Adam's vision of heavenly things faded; and he and his descendants grew inordinately attached to earthly things.

God's love for fallen mankind caused Him to send His own Divine Son made Man, to redeem man by His cruel death on the cross. Christ paid our ransom in full, fastening our sins to the cross (Col. 2:14). Through baptism we were made adopted children and heirs to the kingdom of God.

At this funeral Mass today, we honor and reverence the mortal remains of _____, because since baptism, his (her) soul, while persevering in the state of grace, was the temple of the living God (2 Cor. 6:16). This body was a living ciborium for the Body, Blood, Soul, and Divinity of Christ when He came to him (her) in Holy Communion. Small wonder, then, that we bless, pray over and incense it, and offer the Holy Sacrifice for the repose of his (her) soul.

Conclusion

Dear friends, do not let sadness blind us to what happened at the moment of _____'s death. His (Her) spiritual and immortal soul, the ultimate principle of his (her) conscious life, the principle by which all human beings feel, think, and will, was called home by God its creator. The human soul is one of God's wondrous creations. It is a simple substance, not composed of parts, and it is a spiritual substance whose existence is independent of matter. God creates every human soul directly at the moment when it is to be united to a body produced by generation to form with that body one human nature. When, by the will of God, the soul, the principle of life, is separated from the body, death results.

Our faith tells us that _____'s soul has "gone home" to be with God. His (Her) soul has "stepped westward," leaving his (her) body behind for awhile—but he (she) lives.

When Christ rose from the dead, He vanquished death. With all your heart and soul, say at this Mass: "I believe in the resurrection of the body and life everlasting"; and that act of faith will bring resignation and a great serenity of heart.

EIGHTH HOMILY

For a funeral with sad circumstances

Extension of sympathy to the family

Introduction

The pages of Holy Scripture are damp with tears shed over the passing of loved ones. For instance, there is the moving passage in the first book of the Bible about Abraham's grief over the death of his beloved wife, Sarah. "Abraham came," Holy Writ tells us, "to mourn and weep for her" (Gen. 23:2). When God's faithful servant Moses died, Scripture records: "For thirty days the Israelites wept for Moses in the plains of Moab" (Deut. 34:8). When Abner was buried in Hebron, it is recorded in the Bible that King David "wept aloud at the grave of Abner, and the people also wept" (2 Sam. 3:32). And who can forget the bitter tears shed by King David at receiving the word of the death of his errant son Absalom. The Bible tells us: "The King was shaken, and went up to the room over the city gate to weep. He said as he wept, 'My son Absalom! My son, my son Absalom! If only I had died instead of you, Absalom, my son, my son' " (2 Sam. 19:1).

Men weep reluctantly. They seek to hide their tears and cover their heads, as David did. A tiny room suffices for their heart-gnawing sorrow. A small room over a city gate served David's need.

Application

Turning to the New Testament, we come upon the moving scene of our Lord Jesus Christ just outside Bethany en route to visit the home of Martha and Mary four days after the death of their beloved brother Lazarus. Scripture, in minute detail, sets down this account of Martha's moving meeting with our Lord on the road to Bethany. Martha, having heard that Christ was coming, went out to meet Him, and said: "Lord, if you had been here, my brother would not have died." Christ assured her that her brother would rise again, proclaiming that He was "the resurrection and the life," and that "whoever believes in me, though he should die, will come to life." Hearing this, Martha went back for Mary who had remained at home, telling her that "the Teacher is here, asking for you."

Making haste, Mary went to where Jesus was, fell at His feet, and said what both she and her sister had been saying for four days: "Lord, if you had been here, my brother would never have died." When Jesus saw Mary weeping, and those who had come with her also weeping, Scripture says that our Lord was "moved by the deepest emotion." He asked, "Where have you laid him?" " 'Lord, come and see,' . . . and Jesus began to weep" (Jn. 11:35). The raising of Lazarus from the dead sealed our Lord's fate. "From that day on there was a plan afoot to kill him" (Jn. 11:53).

Let us who are present at this funeral Mass for the repose of the soul of _____, remember that Christ was true Man and true God. As Man, He had all the emotions we have; and He was moved to tears at the sorrow inflicted on Martha and Mary by the death of their revered brother and His beloved friend. Christ, better than any of us here, will understand our sorrow and tears. He who made us all, knows the therapy of tears. It is clear that Ovid also knew it, or why would he write: "It is some relief to weep; grief is satisfied and carried off by tears"?

Conclusion

Dear friends, I repeat, our Lord will understand the tears of the family and friends today; but what He will not understand is a grief that borders on despair or one that is prolonged beyond reasonable bounds. At no time is the exercise of faith more sorely needed than on the occasion of the death of a loved one. As true followers of Christ, we must believe in the resurrection of our Lord Jesus from the dead on Easter Sunday, and in the resurrection of the bodies of all human beings at the end of the world. We profess these articles of faith when we say the Apostles' Creed, when we join in the Profession of Faith at all Sunday and Holy-Day Masses and in any one of the four proclamations of the mystery of faith immediately following the consecration of the bread and wine into the Body, Blood, Soul and Divinity of Christ.

No one has a right to question the will of God. Like Job, we must say: "The LORD gave and the LORD has taken away; blessed be the name of the LORD" (Job. 1:21). Not one of us has the right, in the face of sorrow, to ask: "Why did this have to happen to us?" unless we have had the habit of asking that same question when the good and joyful things of life came to us from the hands of God.

Merciful Lord, receive the soul of _____. Grant him (her) your favor and the gift of eternal glory.

NINTH HOMILY

General

Extension of sympathy to the family

Introduction

The final chapter of the Book of Deuteronomy records the death of the incomparable Moses. Here was a man who had seen more of the glory of God than any other Old Testament saint, a man to whom God spoke "mouth to mouth and plainly" (Num. 12:8). At the age of one hundred and twenty years, God let him know that the time for his submission to the universal law of death was at hand. The Lord said to Moses:

> Go up on Mount Nebo, here in the Abarim Mountains . . . and view the land of Canaan which I am giving to the Israelites as their possession. Then you shall die on the mountain you have climbed . . . You may indeed view the land at a distance, but you shall not enter that land which I am giving to the Israelites (Deut. 32:49,50,52).

The Lord had said of Moses that he was "the meekest man on the face of the earth" (Num. 12:3), and the Patriarch proved his meekness by making no protest over being excluded from entering the Promised Land with the Chosen People he had brought out of Egypt. There was total submission to God's will on the part of Moses.

Again, there was the matter of the place of his death, a lonely spot on Mount Nebo; and the circumstance of dying alone, separated from the people he had led for forty years of the Exodus, did not concern him. God had called Moses his "servant"; as such he would be obedient unto death. In the Latin Vulgate version of the death of Moses, we read these moving lines:

> And Moses, the servant of the Lord, died, in the land of Moab, by the commandment of the Lord. And he buried him in the valley of the land of Moab over against Phogor (Deut. 34:5–6).

What a magnificent tribute to the great Patriarch Moses, that the Lord Himself, perhaps through the ministry of the angels, directed his burial in a spot known only to God.

Application

My dear friends, I see certain parallels between the passing of Moses and the passing of _____. He (She) was also a servant of God who strove to fulfill the end of his (her) creation, one who did his (her) best to fulfill the duties of his (her) state in life with uncommon fidelity. His (Her) devotion to his (her) religious obligations to God, to the Church, and to his (her) neighbors was outstanding, setting for all of us an example hard to follow and difficult to surpass. Again, like Moses, he (she) saw in death a "commandment of the Lord" and faced it with heroic calmness, seeing in the malaise preceding it the will of God.

Should his (her) immortal soul, because of human frailties not completely atoned for during life, be deterred from entering heaven for a time, he (she) counts on our prayers, Masses, and Holy Communions, to shorten that time by suffrages offered to God in his (her) behalf. The Word of God assures us: "It is a holy and wholesome thought to pray for the dead that they be loosed from their sins" (2 Mach. 12:46). St. Augustine would say that it is not to be doubted that the dead are aided by the prayers of the Church and the salutary Sacrifice of the Mass, and by alms given in suffrage to the poor in their behalf, "that the Lord may deal with them more mercifully than their sins deserve. For this, which has been handed down by the Fathers, the universal Church observes." St. Augustine's own mother, St. Monica, elicited this promise on her deathbed: "One thing only I ask you, that you remember me at the altar of the Lord wherever you may be." _____ elicits this same promise from his (her) family, relatives, and friends.

Finally, there is one more parallel one can draw between the death and burial of Moses and that of _____. The committal of the mortal remains of Moses was under the direction of God Himself. That was not a special privilege reserved only for His servant Moses. Be comforted in the knowledge that God is intimately involved in this funeral today. Is it not taking place in God's house? Will not God's Divine Son be present on the altar after the consecration offering Himself to His Father, pleading pardon, mercy, and eternal rest for _____? And will not God's angels also minister at the graveside, since the priest can call on them to guard the grave until the resurrection? Let us praise God for His mercy!

Conclusion

With all my heart, I pronounce over the mortal remains of _____ the very blessing God taught Moses to utter over the Chosen People:

> The Lord bless you and keep you. The Lord let his face shine upon you, and be gracious to you. The Lord look upon you kindly and give you peace (Num. 6:24–26).

TENTH HOMILY

General

Extension of sympathy to the family

Introduction

It is said that people who visit the grave of Lord Baden-Powell, the famous founder of the Boy Scout organizations around the world, come away impressed by the simplicity of his tombstone in the East African cemetery where he lies buried. It is inscribed:

> Lord Baden-Powell, Chief Scout of the world, Born February 22nd., 1857, died January 8th., 1941.

Beneath the inscription is a circle with a dot in the center of it.

The circle and the dot in the center were a mystery to many persons until an authority on scouting remembered that Lord Baden-Powell had, to get the organization started, put together a small book, a manual, in which the author had included some basic signs and symbols to help beginners. One of the symbols was the circle and the dot. It seems that when the founder took a troop of scouts on a hike, he always went on ahead, marking dangerous spots, springs with safe drinking water, and safe paths to follow. At the point where the hike was to terminate, there would be found a sign with the circle and the dot in the center. It meant: "I have gone home."

Application

To St. Peter, the first Vicar of Christ on earth, death was simply a matter of "going home." There was no panic upon learning from our Lord Himself that the end of his earthly sojourn was approaching. He put it this way:

> I know, by the indications our Lord Jesus Christ has given me, how close is the day when I must fold my tent. I shall press to have you recall these things frequently after my departure (2 Pet. 1:14–15).

First, note the term St. Peter used to describe his mortal body. He called it a "tent." Other translations of the New Testament use the word "tabernacle" in as much as God, by a special presence, dwells in the soul of every baptized Christian in the state of grace. Hear our Lord say: "Anyone who loves me will be true to my word; and my Father will love him; we will come to him and make our dwelling place with him" (Jn. 14:23).

The Apostle Paul asks: "Are you not aware that you are the temple of God and that the Spirit of God dwells in you?" (I Cor. 3:16) Pressing home this truth, he again writes: "You must know that your body is a temple of the Holy Spirit, who is within—the Spirit you received from

God. You are not your own. You have been purchased, and at a price. So glorify God in your body" (I Cor. 6:19–20).

The Scripture passages just quoted supply the answer to the question frequently asked: "Why do Catholics pay so much respect to the mortal remains of their dead?" It is because we believe that the body of the deceased was a tent, temple, or tabernacle in which God dwelt while the person was alive. Small wonder, then, that the mortal remains of _____ will be prayed over, blessed with holy water and incensed, since it is holy to God, to the Church, and to the family, in as much as it too, rendered worship to God.

> A second point to be considered, is, that knowing his death was imminent, St. Peter continued his apostolic ministry to the end. In this, he was like St. Paul, who taught: "The general rule is that each one should lead the life the Lord has assigned to him continuing as he was when the Lord called him." (1 Cor. 7:17). _____ obeyed St. Paul's rule to the very end of his (her) life. He (She) sought to discharge all the duties of the state of life assigned him (her) by the Creator. He (She) has gone to garner his (her) eternal rewards.

Finally, there was St. Peter's complete surrender to God's Will concerning the time, place, and circumstances of his death. He longed to go "home to God." St. Peter never forgot his experience on Mount Tabor when our Lord was transfigured before his eyes. He mentioned it in the last Epistle he wrote: "For we were eyewitnesses of his sovereign majesty. He received glory and praise from God the Father when that unique declaration came to him out of the majestic splendor: 'This is my beloved Son, on whom my favor rests.' We ourselves heard this said from heaven while we were in his company on the holy mountain" (2 Pet. 1:17–18). Seeing Christ in His majestic glory gave St. Peter such a longing to go home to be with God in heaven that the cruel pains of his crucifixion were sweet to him.

Conclusion

Who can say for certain that our Lord did not show His merciful countenance to _____ during his (her) last sufferings? There was a resignation that makes one feel that there is profound truth in the breviary antiphon which says: "We are happy to be chastened by God, who heals us as he wounds."

The inscription on the tomb of President Garfield might very well form an epitaph for _____. It reads:

> Life's race well run,
> Life's work well done,
> Life's crown well won,
>   Now comes rest.

ELEVENTH HOMILY

For a charitable widow

Extension of sympathy to the family

Introduction

St. Mark, the Evangelist, tells us in his Gospel how, one day, our Lord seated Himself opposite the treasury in the temple area and watched as the different people approached to make their contributions. It is said that there were ten or twelve trumpet-shaped metal receptacles, each duly marked to indicate the purpose for which the funds would be used. Naturally, when many coins were deposited, quite a sound was generated. So, there was our Lord watching with interest the actions of the donors, and listening to the sound of the coins as they dropped into the receptacles.

While our Lord watched, He noticed a woman approaching the votive stands and saw her put in two small copper coins worth a few cents. Christ called His disciples over and told them: "I want you to observe that this poor widow has contributed more than all the others who donated to the treasury. They gave from their surplus wealth, but she gave from her want, all that she had to live on" (Mk. 12:43–44).

Nothing is hidden from God. Christ knew that the woman was a widow, that her offering consisted of but two copper coins, and that the offering she made was all she had to live on. The two copper coins did not make much sound when they were dropped into the receptacle, but the echo of them has resounded down through the centuries, and will continue to do so, wherever St. Mark's Gospel is read.

Application

In the Old Testament, widows and orphans were accorded special reverence and protection by order of God Himself: "You shall not wrong any widow or orphan. If you ever wrong them and they cry out to me, I will surely hear their cry. My wrath will flare up" (Exod. 22:21–23). In the New Testament, there is the moving account of our Lord as an infant being brought to the temple in Jerusalem by His mother and foster father for the ritual presentation according to the law of Moses. There were two strangers in their golden years present for the ceremony. One was Simeon, a "just and pious man" who awaited the coming of the Messiah. He was there under the inspiration of the Holy Spirit, who had told him that he would not die until he had seen the Promised One. Taking the infant Jesus in his arms, Simeon blessed God and said: "Now, Master, you can dismiss your servant in peace; you have fulfilled your word" (Lk. 2:36–38).

The other privileged person was a widow, the prophetess Anna, who was eighty-four. Scripture says of her that "she was constantly in the temple worshiping God every day and night in fasting and in prayer." She became the herald of the coming of the Messiah, for she talked about the Divine Child to all who were looking for the promised Redeemer (Lk. 2:36–38).

Conclusion

Dear friends, we are gathered here this morning for the offering of the Holy Sacrifice of the Mass for the repose of the soul of Mrs. _____, a woman loved and cherished by her family and highly respected by her neighbors and friends. We would be in error if we entertained for a moment the thought that life has ended for Mrs. _____. It has not ended. It has just begun. Death came when her Creator called forth her spiritual and immortal soul, the principle of life in all of us, by which we feel, think, will, and remember. Her soul, since it is a simple, spiritual, and immortal substance, has an existence independent of matter. It is her soul that has gone on ahead to God. Her mortal remains honored here today will, as Christ told us, rise from the grave on the last day. Soul and body will be reunited on that day. This must be our firm belief. "Without faith," said then Archbishop Joseph Bernardin of Chicago, "death is both obscene and absurd."

When I think of Mrs. _____, I remember her outstanding devotion to the Blessed Sacrament, her prayerful visits to the church when she was able, and her constant prayers at home; I am reminded of the widow Anna, who prayed night and day in the temple, and who, by word and example, spoke to all of a "loving and merciful God."

Too, when I think of Mrs. _____, I recall her generous work for the parish (and the school?). Through the years, when volunteers were needed for parochial or charitable works, she would be among the first to offer her services. When age and health hampered her activities, she was like the widow Christ praised for her generosity. She, too, may have given to the parish and to charities from her need.

I feel I would not be far from the truth to say of Mrs. _____ that she put into her life, (her family?), her parish, all she had to give—herself!

God give her eternal rest!

TWELFTH HOMILY

General

Extension of sympathy to the family

Introduction

When Lazarus, a family friend of our Lord, fell sick, his sisters, Mary and Martha, sent word to Him couched in these touching words: "Lord, the one you love is sick." The Master's comment upon receipt of the message was: "This sickness is not to end in death; but that through it the Son of God may be glorified" (Jn. 11:4).

After delaying the journey to Bethany, Christ said to His disciples: "Our beloved Lazarus has fallen asleep, but I am going there to wake him." The disciples remarked: "Lord, if he is asleep, his life will be saved." The inspired writer explains that the disciples thought that, when our Lord spoke of His cherished friend as being asleep, He meant sleep in the sense of slumber. Our Lord spoke to them plainly, "Lazarus is dead" (Jn. 11:11–16).

Death is frequently referred to as a "sleep" in the New Testament. In the account of the cruel martyrdom of St. Stephen by stoning, these words detail the saint's execution: "And falling on his knees, he [Stephen] cried with a loud voice, saying, 'Lord, do not hold this sin against them.' And when he had said this, he fell asleep in the Lord" (Acts 7:59).

St. Paul, the Apostle to the Gentiles, made use of the word *sleep* in reference to death twice in his First Epistle to the Corinthians, and twice in his First Epistle to the Thessalonians. For instance, in instructing his converts concerning the resurrection of our Lord from the dead on Easter Sunday, the Apostle cited the fact that more than five hundred persons had seen the Risen Christ at one time and that "most of them are still alive, although some have fallen asleep" (1 Cor. 15:6). St. Peter, also, in his Second Epistle, refers to the dead as having gone to their rest (2 Pet. 3:4).

Application

The sleep of death must be understood as referring to the body alone, and not to the soul. Applied to the body, it is a comforting thought, signifying rest from pain, weariness, and the worries of this world. The soul, however, does not sleep. The continuing activity of the soul after death is clear from the words of St. Paul, that we should "rather be away from the body and at home with the Lord" (2 Cor. 5:8). Released from the body, the soul actually becomes more active.

Having shared in a limited way in God's own life through sanctifying grace received in baptism, or when it is restored through the sacrament of penance, or by an act of perfect contrition after its loss by grave sin, the released soul will receive the *"lumen gloriae*—the light of glory."￼ Pope Benedict XII, in 1336, defined in his Bull *Benedictus Deus* that those who die in the state of sanctifying grace "behold the Divine Essence intuitively and face to face." This incomparable gift empowers the soul to share, in varying degrees, in the boundless vision of God, the Beatific Vision. "We shall be like him," says St. John, "because we shall see him as he is" (1 Jn. 3:2). The acts which compose the heavenly blessedness are knowledge, love, and joy.

It is a common teaching of the Church that in addition to the essential bliss of heaven which springs from the immediate Beatific Vision of God, there is also an accessory blessedness which proceeds from natural knowledge and love of created things. This accessory bliss is achieved by the blessed souls in heaven in virtue of the community of life with Christ, with our Blessed Mother Mary, with the angels and saints, and in virtue of their reunion with saved members of their families and former friends from the time of earthly life.

Conclusion

My dear friends, in spite of our feelings of loss, I am sure that not one person here, if he or she had the power to do so, would call back _____ from the dead to have him (her) endure again the trials and sufferings of this life and have to die a second time. Who among us could be so selfish as to think only of ourselves and deprive the dear departed of his (her) rest, peace, and joy in heaven with God? St. Paul got a brief vision of what he termed the "third heaven"; and he was so overcome by the revelation that he wrote: "Eye has not seen, nor ear heard, neither has it entered into the heart of man the things God has prepared for those who love him" (1 Cor. 2:9).

Small wonder that the Little Flower of Jesus could say to those around her deathbed: "I am not dying; I am entering into life." _____ _____ has entered into life. May he (she) remember our needs before the throne of God.

May all the faithful departed, through the mercy of God, rest in peace. Amen.

THIRTEENTH HOMILY

General

Extension of sympathy to the family

Introduction

When Dr. S. B. Leakey (1903–1972), the famous African anthropologist, suffered a fall from a lecture platform, he tried to pass it off as nothing, saying that he had "nine lives." The truth was that the injury was serious, and his recovery was slow. He did become impatient over the length of his convalescence and was heard to say that "he was a prisoner in his own body."

One day some friends paid him a visit, and somehow the conversation turned to religion and death. Leakey, son of English missionary parents, when asked what he thought of death, opened his eyes wide, stared into space, and replied: "Death—why should I bother about that? Only my flesh and bones will die, but I shall go on living forever."

Application

We stand in admiration and reverential awe in the presence of those who face death without exaggerated fear or panic. Not infrequently, God has to act with some as He did with Lot in Sodom, plucking them away against their will. Not so with _____. Close relatives and friends who loved him (her) and visited during his (her) last illness were comforted by his (her) noble courage and resignation. He (She) set a fine example to family and strangers alike by his (her) Christian life, and, in dying, taught them how to face death with faith, resignation, and dignity.

In death, the soul seeks its freedom to enter into the kingdom of heaven with God, while the body submits to the universal decree of its Maker and returns to the dust from which it came. Had Adam not sinned, there would never have been a scene like this anywhere in the world!

Death shifts the burden to the loved ones left behind. The pangs of loss, the loneliness, the emptiness of life without the departed one, may become at times unbearable. Believe me, God understands our sorrow and tears, but what He will not understand is a grief that borders on rebellion. St. Jerome brings this out well in the attempt he made to console St. Paula when her daughter, Blesilla, died. In a letter to St. Paula, St. Jerome reminded her that she ought to be afraid that God would be offended by the intensity of her grief, since it reflected on God's love and His judgment, and that, St. Jerome said, would be outrageous. "When I think you are a mother," wrote St. Jerome, "I do not blame you for weeping; but when I think of you as a Christian, I wish the Christian in you would comfort the mother in you."

Conclusion

Dear family and relatives, our hearts go out to you at this trying time. In the face of death, only an angel could have asked Mary Magdalene as she stood outside the tomb of our Blessed Lord: "Woman, why are you weeping?" An angel might well have been excused for asking such a question, since no angel ever had to part with a loved one, or know the bitter loss of someone near and dear. This in no way means that angels do not sympathize with human beings in their sorrow. In this particular case of Mary Magdalene weeping at the tomb, there was no need for the two bright angelic messengers to express sympathy, since they were there to announce the glad tidings of Christ's glorious resurrection.

It is comforting to realize that the first recorded words of the Risen Christ were to Mary Magdalene, the converted sinner. When she saw our Lord standing there, she did not recognize Him. He asked her two questions: "Woman, why are you weeping?" and "Who is it you are looking for?" She, thinking He was the gardener, said: "Sir, if you are the one who carried him off, tell me where you have laid him and I will take him away." When our Lord found that His cruel death on the cross, which Mary Magdalene personally witnessed on Calvary, had not dimmed her faith, that the empty tomb had not drained her of courage, and that her sorrow had not extinguished her hope, He said to her, "Mary!" She turned to Him and said, in a frenzy of love, one word in Hebrew, "Rabboni!" (meaning "Teacher") (Jn. 20:11–16). The second question of our Lord: "Who is it you are looking for?" required no answer. Reporting to the disciples, Mary Magdalene made her profession of faith: "I have seen the Lord!" (Jn. 20:18).

Indeed, _____ lives, and by virtue of a special grace, participates in God's knowledge, life, and love for all eternity. On our part, if we love him (her), we must let him (her) go. Sorrow is a price we all must pay for love!

FOURTEENTH HOMILY

For a young girl

Expression of sympathy to the family

Introduction

There is a moving incident related in St. Mark's Gospel concerning the grief of a father over the grave illness of his only child, a twelve-year-old daughter. Somehow he had heard of the miracles Christ had performed for the sick: he sought Him out and found Him in the midst of a large crowd. He worked his way through until he came before Christ. Falling down before Him, Jairus, a ruler of the synagogue, entreated Him to come to his house, saying: "My little daughter is critically ill. Please come and lay your hands on her so that she may get well and live" (Mk. 5:23).

If Jairus needed further confirmation of Christ's divine power, right there in the crowd was a woman who for twelve long years had suffered from a continuing hemorrhage. Holy Scripture says of her: "She had received treatment at the hands of doctors of every sort, and exhausted her savings in the process, yet she got no relief; on the contrary, she only got worse" (Mk. 5:26). With a faith born of desperation, that woman managed to get near our Lord and slyly reach out her hand and touch His cloak: "Immediately her flow of blood dried up and the feeling that she was cured of her affliction ran through her whole body" (Mk. 5:29). Our Lord told her that it was her faith that had healed her.

While Christ was still talking to the woman, someone came from the house of the ruler of the synagogue, saying to Jairus: "Your daughter is dead. Why bother the Teacher further?" Christ, hearing what had been said to the bereaved father, said to him: "Fear is useless. What is needed is trust." Upon reaching the house of Jairus, our Lord encountered a tumult of weeping and wailing people. He asked them why they were "making such a din with their wailing." Then he said: "The child is not dead. She is asleep." Those who had prepared the child for burial laughed him to scorn.

Clearing the house of mourners, Christ took only the parents and three Apostles into the room where the child lay. Taking her cold little hand in His, our Lord said: "Little girl, get up." "The girl, a child of twelve, stood up immediately and began to walk around . . . and they were utterly amazed. And he charged them strictly that no one should know of it, and directed that something be given to the little girl to eat" (Mk. 5:41–43).

Application

If there was ever a time when one needs faith, it is in the presence of death, but, more especially, of the death of a child. We note in the Gospel account of the death of Jairus' daughter, that she was but twelve years of age and that she was an only child, circumstances that point up the stark tragedy of her passing; nevertheless, our Blessed Lord demanded faith and trust on the part of her father: "Fear is useless. What is needed is trust." The same Christ who said those words to Jairus is present now in the tabernacle; and in a few moments He will be present on the altar after the words of Consecration, a Victim offering Himself to His Eternal Father for the living and the dead. To each of us here this morning, Christ says: "What is needed is trust."

Conclusion

Dear parents, call to mind God's wondrous love for your daughter. From all eternity she was in His divine mind. He knew the year, the month, day, and hour of her birth and her falling asleep. He was the creator of her soul and body. Every mother who ever brought a child into this world has to say with the mother of the Maccabees: "I know not how you were formed in my womb; for I neither gave you breath, nor soul; neither did I frame the limbs of any one of you" (2 Macc. 7:22). As her creator, God had first claim on her. Part of God's goodness to her was in confiding her to the loving care of good parents who would be His worthy representatives on earth.

Say not in your heart that God has done an injustice in taking _____ to Himself. Say, rather, what Job said upon learning of the tragic deaths of his seven children, all at one time. Falling to the ground and worshiping God, he said: "The LORD gave and the LORD has taken away; blessed be the name of the LORD" (Job 1:21).

Only a tender and merciful God would, after restoring life to a dead child, think of ordering food for her. Does anyone here think that our God would be unmindful of all the desires of little _____? Indeed not. With God she has peace and love, and these she would not exchange for all the treasures in this world. She has God, and He is love itself!

FIFTEENTH HOMILY

General

Expression of sympathy to the family

Introduction

In the Old Testament Book of Judges it is recorded that Gideon, with only three hundred men, overcame an army of Midianites and Amalekites "as numerous as a plague of grasshoppers and whose camels were without number."

Gideon divided his army into three companies of one hundred men each, and placed in each man's right hand a trumpet, and in his left hand a lamp hidden in an earthen pitcher. Under cover of darkness, the three hundred soldiers surrounded the enemy camp. Upon a given signal by Gideon, the trumpets were sounded and the earthen pitchers were broken to reveal the lighted lamps. The enemies panicked and began to kill each other with their own swords; and as Scripture says, "the whole camp fell to running, shouting and fleeing" (Judg. 7:21).

Application

The passing away of _____ could be compared to the breaking of the earthen vessels surrounding the lighted torches in the hands of Gideon's soldiers. Death is the breaking of the earthen vessel (the body), freeing the soul to soar into the eternal light of God's glory. It is in this context that St. Paul refers to the body as an "earthen vessel." Hear St. Paul say: "Indeed, we know that when the earthly tent (body) in which we dwell is destroyed, we have a dwelling provided for us by God, a dwelling in the heavens, not made by hands but to last forever" (2 Cor. 5:1).

For St. Paul, death was an essential gateway to eternal life; he asserted that, while we are in the body, we are absent from the Lord; and then he personalized his belief in these words: "For to me 'life' means Christ; hence dying is so much gain . . . I long to be freed from this life and to be with Christ, for that is the far better thing" (Phil. 1:23–24).

In the case of the death of a person well advanced in years, or of one whose illness was protracted, or of one who suffered great agony, we can say more easily: "Thank God He took him or her." But should the person taken be young or middle-aged, this may be considered a stark tragedy, even, to some, an injustice. To everyone in the state of grace, death must be considered an inestimable gain. To think otherwise is to be guilty of ignorance as to the nature of the soul.

Man is made up of two essential parts, a material body and a spiritual soul, the soul being an immediate creation by God. We know the soul is spiritual because some of its actions are independent of matter. Again, the soul is spiritual in that it moves and directs itself, as it does, in the exercise of free will. Since the spiritual soul acts independently of the body, it can exist when it is separated from the body. When the soul is withdrawn from the body, "the spiritual element survives and subsists after death, an element with consciousness and will so that the 'human self' subsists."*

How truly the Church can say in the Preface of this very Mass:

> The sadness of death gives way to the bright promise of immortality. Lord, for your faithful people life is changed, but not ended. When the body of our earthly dwelling lies in death, we gain an everlasting dwelling place in heaven.

Pious writers have said that, were any of us privileged to see a human soul in the state of grace, we would be so overcome by its dazzling beauty that we would lose consciousness. Saints who have seen holy souls en route to their rendezvous with God remarked about the great light which enveloped them, rivaling the sun in brightness. Pope St. Gregory the Great relates in his writings how Venerable Bennet, being a long distance from Capua, at midnight, beheld the soul of Germanus, bishop of Capua, being transported to heaven in a globe of brilliant light.

Conclusion

Power, greatness, and light are descriptive words often found in Holy Scripture in relation to God. For instance, in the Old Testament, Isaiah said in prophecy: "The LORD shall be your light forever" (Isa. 60:19). When our Lord became Man, He proclaimed: "I am the light of the world. No follower of mine shall ever walk in darkness; no, he shall possess the light of life" (Jn. 8:12).

It should console us all that the gentle soul of _____ has gone into the presence of God. The Book of Revelation tells us of the saved:

> They shall see him [God] face to face and bear his name on their foreheads. The night shall be no more. They will need no light from lamps or the sun, for the Lord God shall give them light, and they shall reign forever (Rev. 22:4–5).

Eternal rest grant unto him (her), O Lord, and let perpetual light shine upon him (her). May he (she) rest in peace. Amen.

---

*From the "Letter on Certain Questions Concerning Eschatology," from the Sacred Congregation for the Doctrine of the Faith, dated May 17, 1979, and released July 14, 1979.

SIXTEENTH HOMILY

For a charitable woman

Extension of sympathy to the family
Introduction

The Acts of the Apostles tells how St. Peter, on a visit to the "saints" who dwelt in Lydda, found a man named Aeneas, a paralytic, who had been bedridden for eight years. St. Peter said to him: "Aeneas, the Lord Jesus Christ cures you. Get up and make your bed." The man got up at once (Acts 9:32–35). St. Luke, the author of the book, adds that all the inhabitants of Lydda and Sharon, upon seeing the man walking around, were converted to the Lord.

There is little doubt but that the news of the miracle spread to Joppa, where a kind and generous woman named Tabitha (in Greek, Dorcas, meaning a gazelle) had fallen ill and died. Tabitha was renowned for her good works and almsdeeds, and her passing was a severe blow to the needy. There was no shortage of women to prepare her mortal remains for burial or mourn her loss at her wake in the upper chamber of her home.

Knowing that St. Peter was at Lydda, two messengers were dispatched to tell him of the death of Tabitha and begged him to come back with them to Joppa; and he did as they asked. Arriving in Joppa, St. Peter went directly to the deceased woman's home and to the upper chamber. Scripture records: "All the widows came to him in tears, and showed him the various garments Tabitha had made for them when she was still with them" (Acts 9:39).

After dismissing the mourners from the room, St. Peter knelt down and prayed. "Turning to the dead body, he said: 'Tabitha, stand up.' She opened her eyes and looked at Peter and sat up. He gave her his hand and helped her to her feet." The next thing he did was to call in those who were believers, and the widows, to show them that she was alive. This became known all over Joppa, and because of it, many came to believe in the Lord. Thus it happened that Peter stayed on in Joppa for a considerable time at the house of Simon, a tanner of leather" (Acts 9:40–43).

Application

Strange, isn't it, how a single striking incident can give a place historical renown. For instance, who would ever think of Runnymede today had the Magna Charta not been signed there in 1215 A.D.? On the other hand, the ancient city of Joppa on the Mediterranean coast had multiple claims to fame. The city is mentioned in many ancient classical writings. It is mentioned in Holy Scripture as the port from which the cedars of Lebanon were shipped for the building of the Temple in Jerusalem. Again, Joppa was the city to which Jonah was heading in his futile attempt to evade God's will. All other claims to greatness, however, were overshadowed by the great miracle performed in Joppa by St. Peter—the raising of Tabitha from the dead.

Tabitha was a remarkable woman, distinguished for her great and active benevolence to the fatherless and the sorrowing widows. Early biblical history shows clearly how God had granted widows a special protection in law, as we note in Exodus and Deuteronomy. In the New Testament, St. Paul evolved a role for widows in caring for the religious and social needs of the poor. That was Tabitha's role. She bent all her energies to imitate God's philanthropy and extend the glory of His name by illustrating the excellence of God-like charity. The greatest tribute to Tabitha was when the widows she had befriended all stood about weeping and showing St. Peter "the various garments Tabitha had made them" (Acts 9:39).

Conclusion

My dear friends, we have gathered here this morning to join in offering the Holy Sacrifice of Mass for the repose of the soul of _____. She deserves our prayers. If any woman deserves the title "another Tabitha," it is _____. Her many charities, her kindness to others, are well known to all of us. No call upon her time or energy was considered a burden to her; rather, she was delighted to be asked. If there was a need, she responded as well as she could. If there was a task, she, more often than not, volunteered.

May the Lord, who heard St. Peter's prayer for Tabitha, hear our fervent prayers at this funeral Mass for _____, and grant her eternal rest.

SEVENTEENTH HOMILY

General

Extension of sympathy to the family

Introduction

Ever since we were tiny children, we were brought to the chruch by our parents; and when we were old enough, we came on our own, to receive the sacramental ashes on Ash Wednesday. As the priest placed the ashes on the forehead, we heard him say: "Remember, man, that you are dust, and into dust you shall return!"

Somehow, the full impact of those words never strikes us with such awful force as when we have to stand and gaze upon the mortal remains of a loved one, as you in the family have had to do these last days. The relationship of the death of _____ to the sin of our first parents is so terribly remote; nevertheless, this funeral Mass today is proof positive that the universal law of God concerning the death of all human beings is still in force. After the devastating fall of Adam, God said to him: "By the sweat of your face shall you get your bread to eat, until you return to the ground from which you were taken; for you are dust, and to dust you shall return" (Gen. 3:19).

Application

There is great consolation in the stirring teaching of the Council Fathers of Vatican II, that in spite of the sin of Adam,

> God has called man and still calls him so that with his entire being he might be joined to him in an endless sharing of a divine life beyond corruption. Christ won this victory when he rose to life, since by his death he freed man from death.

Because of Adam's sin, the earth has a claim, for a time, on the body of man since it was made from it; but the soul is made in the image and likeness of God, and infused from above; and God takes the spiritual, immortal soul of the just man to Himself.

The soul, the principle of life, has been called by God, and we have every reason to hope and pray that it has gone into heaven where it continues to live in happiness. At the end of the world, there will be the resurrection of all the dead, among them, the body of _____ _____. His (Her) soul will be reunited with his (her) body present here this morning, never again to know separation.

The mortal remains of _____ will surely rise from the grave on the last day. This is an article of faith. Have we not professed this faith every time we have recited the Apostles' Creed: "I believe . . . in the resurrection of the body"? Did not the third of the seven sons, whose martyrdom is heralded in the Old Testament Second Book of Maccabees, offer his tongue and his hands to his executioners with this exalted profession of faith: "It was from heaven that I received these; for the sake of his laws I disdain them; from him I hope to receive them again" (2 Macc. 7:11).

In the New Testament we read how our Lord frequently* taught the resurrection of the body, and chided the Sadducees for their denial of it because of their ignorance of the Scriptures. Christ called Himself "the resurrection and the life" and said that "whoever believes in me, though he should die, will come to life" (Jn. 11:26).

The Fourth Lateran Council in 1215 declared that "all men shall rise again with their own bodies, which they now bear, to receive according to their works." St. Thomas says, "Man will rise again in the greatest possible natural perfection" (Suppl., 81:1).

The dogma of the resurrection of the body teaches a real and complete resurrection of man in the fullness of his nature. There is a threefold identity in the risen man which makes him the same person he was from birth: (1) identity of soul, (2) identity of bodily life, and (3) identity of the ultimate material substance of the body. The resurrection of the dead is a tribute to God's omnipotence; that the risen body is endowed with spiritual and supernatural qualities is a further tribute to God's goodness. For instance, the Gospels tell us that the risen body is *immortal* "and cannot die any more" (Lk. 20:36); and that the body of the saved person shall rise in *glory*, "to shine like the sun in the Father's kingdom" (Matt. 13:43).

Conclusion

Dear friends, this Mass being offered this morning benefits the soul of the deceased and should comfort the members of the family. Think of it: after the Consecration at this Mass, Christ, the very Son of God, who Himself died a cruel death, was buried, and rose from the grave, will offer Himself to His Eternal Father as a victim, pleading mercy for _____. He will remind His Father that it was His will that He, the Redeemer, should lose nothing of what He gave Him; rather, that He should raise it up on the last day. Ponder well the words of our Savior:

> Indeed, this is the will of my Father, that every one who looks upon the Son, and believes in him shall have eternal life. Him I will raise up on the last day (Jn. 6:39–40).

Dying, you destroyed our death; rising, you restored our life; Lord Jesus, come in glory. Amen.

---

*See: Matt. 22:29; Mk. 12:18–27; Lk. 20:27–38; Jn. 5:28–29.

EIGHTEENTH HOMILY

General

Extension of sympathy to the family

Introduction

St. Geremarus, before entering the religious life, was married. He was the father of three children—two daughters and one son. His saintly wife and both daughters predeceased him; and when his son was old enough, the father entered a religious order and became such an extraordinary man of prayer that he was, in time, elected abbot.

Perhaps the most effective sermon St. Geremarus ever preached consisted not in words as much as in example. For when his last child and only son Amalbert died, the saint called the monks around him and, kneeling, prayed: "O my God, I thank You that You have shown Your mercy toward me by calling my son to Your glory in heaven." St. Geremarus had given himself totally to God. He had nothing more to give save his beloved son, and he gave him to God with joy and resignation.

Application

My dear friends, for all of us here this morning, the funeral of _____ should be a moving sermon, for as the Council Fathers of Vatican II said: "It is in the face of death that the riddle of human existence becomes most acute." Indeed, death is a riddle; and unless we strive to understand the reason for it, there is no intelligent answer to it.

The first lesson taught by this funeral, and every other funeral, is that sin must be a horrible abomination to God, since the sin of Adam is still a plague to all his descendants. The tears, the awful heartaches caused by the passing away of loved ones, must be laid to Adam's sin, a sin which was by moral nature a sin of disobedience; but the root of the disobedience was pride. "Pride," says Holy Scripture, "is the reservoir of sin" (Sir. 10:13). The sin of Adam, which St. Augustine terms "an inexpressively great sin," is transmitted to his posterity, not by imitation, but by descent, and dwells in every single human being. Adam's sin is called original sin, and the havoc wrought by it beggars description. Our dear Lord's Mother, Mary, alone was preserved from it because of her role as the mother of the Savior of the world.

By original sin, our first parents were deprived of sanctifying grace; and this is, as noted by the Council of Trent, the death of the soul. Along with the loss of sanctifying grace, man's will was weakened and his intellect darkened; as a result, man is subject to concupiscence, suffering, and death. St. Paul teaches in a most definitive manner that death is a consequence of Adam's sin: "Therefore, just as through one man sin entered the world and with sin death, death thus coming to all men inasmuch as all sinned" (Rom. 5:12).

Conclusion

The first lesson, then, that comes to us from a Christian funeral is that sin must be a horrible thing in the sight of God to have caused such devastating consequences for mankind. Our most earnest resolve must be to avoid sin at any cost.

The second lesson to be learned from a Christian funeral is one of hope and consolation. The Council Fathers of Vatican II proclaim:

> The Church has been taught by divine revelation, and herself firmly teaches, that man has been created by God for a blissful purpose beyond the reach of earthly misery . . . that with his entire being he might be joined to him in an endless sharing of a divine life beyond all corruption. Christ won this victory when he rose to life, since by his death he freed man from death.

On this particular occasion it is the resurrection of our Lord from the dead, the victorious completion of the work of redemption, that should lessen the pain of this day. Hear St. Paul say: "But as it is, Christ is now raised from the dead, the first fruits of those who have fallen asleep. Death came through one man; hence, the resurrection of the dead comes through one man. Just as in Adam all die, so in Christ all will come to life again" (1 Cor. 15:20–22).

Two lessons must be learned from this funeral: (1) the enormity of sin that could bring death into the world, and (2) the infinite love of God for man that He would send His Son to suffer and die on the cross to redeem us, to open heaven for us, and "swallow up death in victory" (1 Cor. 15:54). _____ will rise again at the end of the world and be reunited with his (her) soul for all eternity. Tell our Lord Himself at this Mass that you believe in the resurrection of the dead. Christ will be honored by your faith in His word, and He will be your comfort.

Happy are those who have died in the Lord; let them rest from their labors, for their good deeds go with them. Amen.

NINETEENTH HOMILY

General

Extension of sympathy to the family

Introduction

It is said that, when St. Lawrence Justinian was on his deathbed, he caught a glimpse of one of his attendants weeping. Summoning his waning strength, he said: "If you wish to weep, go away; for if you want to remain with me, you must rejoice, as I rejoice, for the gate of heaven is at last opened to me, so that I may be united with my God."

Application

Isn't it a paradox that we would be counseled to rejoice at the passing away of a loved one? Yet, this is what we are asked to do by the Church. The stage is set by the liturgy in present-day funerals: the priest vested in white, flowers on the altar, the lighted Easter candle in the sanctuary, and the casket covered with a white pall, a reminder of the baptismal robe used in the sacrament of baptism. All these things say to us in so many words: "If you wish to weep, go away; for if you want to remain, you must rejoice."

It is this sort of thinking that seems to be behind the custom of celebrating the Christian's day of death as his or her birthday—birth into heaven. Relatively few actual birthdays of the saints become their feast days. To my knowledge, only three birthdays are celebrated in the liturgy: our Lord's birthday on December 25, our Blessed Lady's birthday on September 8, and that of St. John the Baptist on June 24. All the other saints' feast days correspond, more often than not, to the date of their passing from this world. A greater day by far is one's birth into heaven than the day of one's birth into this world.

Birthdays are joyful occasions, with the gifts, the cards, the gathering of relatives and friends, and, of course, the food. In all truth, we who are here today at this funeral Mass for ＿＿＿＿＿＿＿＿＿＿＿ are gathered together to celebrate his (her) birthday into heaven, which, if not immediately attained, shall, we trust, be hastened by this Mass and other Masses, our fervent prayers, and charities done in suffrage in his (her) behalf.

While the mortal remains of the deceased must pay the common penalty of Adam's sin pronounced on all mankind by God, "For you are dust, and to dust you shall return" (Gen. 3:19), those sad words are directed to the body. The soul, if it be in the state of perfect charity, will enter into heavenly bliss. God's great birthday gift to all justified souls on entering heaven, as Pope Benedict XII declared, is to "behold the Divine Essence immediately and face to face, by the Divine Essence offering itself to them, uncovered, clear, and open, and . . . by reason of the Beatific Vision and of this happiness, they are truly blessed and have eternal life and eternal rest."

His Holiness Pope Paul VI in his: The Credo of the People of God, confirms our faith when teaching as follows:

> "We believe in the life eternal. We believe that the souls of all those who die in the grace of Christ, whether they must still be purified in Purgatory, or whether from the moment they leave their bodies Jesus takes them to Paradise as He did for the Good Thief, are the People of God in the eternity beyond death, which will be finally conquered on the day of the resurrection when these souls will be reunited with their bodies."

The souls of the just will enjoy the vision of God in an entirely intellectual way, of a degree that will correspond with the supernatural merits acquired by them during their life. These souls will not be in a state of unconsciousness, but will be fully aware of their own existence, their election, and final escape from all evil. The souls in heaven are members of the Church Triumphant; they are in communion with the Church Suffering—the Holy Souls in Purgatory; and they are in communion with the Church Militant, us here on earth, and they receive our prayers and intercede for us before the throne of God.

Conclusion

At the end of the world, _____'s soul will be reunited to the revered mortal remains being blessed and honored at this Mass. At the resurrection of the dead this body will be perfected by the power of Almighty God to be immortal, and never again to be subject to sickness, pain, or death. The risen body will be a perfection of beauty, and it will shine with clarity and glory.

The third Eucharistic Prayer assures us that all who have left this world in God's friendship hope to share in God's glory and see Him as He is, become like Him and praise Him forever through Christ our Lord.

This is our pious and earnest hope for _____ on his (her) birthday into the kingdom of heaven. Amen.

TWENTIETH HOMILY

General

Extension of sympathy to the family

Introduction

It is said that Arnold Toynbee once facetiously remarked, "Death is an un-American affront to our inalienable right to life, liberty, and the pursuit of happiness." The truth is that, for all true Christians, death is no terminator of life, liberty, or the pursuit of happiness; it is, rather the indispensable key to all three.

Application

Life. The gift of life is a free gift of God. There was a time when neither _____ nor any of us here existed. We came into existence at a time and place of God's choosing, and we leave this world under identical terms. The burning question is, "Why did God create any of us, since He was completely happy and needed nothing to add to His perfection or His happiness?" God, desiring neither a happy solitude nor a lonely beatitude, created spiritual angels, and man, who is a combination of material body and spiritual soul, out of pure love. He wanted to share His happiness with others. As St. Irenaeus said: "God did not create man because He had any need of him, but because He felt the need of some beings upon whom to bestow His gifts."

The catechism sums up the reason why God created us in this answer: "God created us to know, love, and serve Him in this life and to be happy with Him in the next." Our eternal reward or eternal rejection is determined by how well we fulfill the end of our creation. Heaven, you see, must be earned or merited.

Keeping in mind that heaven must be merited, we can understand why the angels were tested and why the faithful ones earned an eternity of bliss in heaven with their Creator, while the rebellious angels went into eternal punishment. Our first parents were tested in the Garden of Eden, and Adam failed the test; and we, his descendants, all share in his guilt through original sin. Death is not the least of the residual effects. Thanks to God's mercy, He had pity on man and He sent His own Divine Son to ransom him by His cruel death on the Cross; and by His resurrection from the dead, He overcame death, saying that all would rise from the grave on the last day. Christ called Himself "the resurrection and the life" (Jn. 11:25); and St. Paul affirmed that "as in Adam all die, so also in Christ all shall be made alive" (1 Cor. 15:22). So death is not the end of living; it is its beginning. Pope Leo XIII said: "God loved us when He gave us life; He loves us also when He takes away this mortal life." For all the faithful, death is the beginning of an eternal life of happiness with God in His kingdom.

Liberty. St. Paul saw liberty and freedom in death. He wrote: "We know that while we dwell in the body we are away from the Lord. We walk by faith, not by sight. I repeat, we are full of confidence and would much rather be away from the body and at home with the Lord" (2 Cor. 5:6–7). Death frees the body from sufferings, illness, loneliness, and the miseries of this world. Death brings freedom to the body and soul. This is vouched for by St. Ambrose: "We know, however, that the soul survives the body, and that, once it is freed from the shackles of its own faculties, it beholds in clear vision what previously, when dwelling in the body, it did not see . . . Therefore, if the death of our flesh frees us from this world, it certainly is no evil, since it restores freedom and excludes pain." Death does not rob us of liberty; rather, it is the key to true freedom.

Pursuit of Happiness. Man is ever pursuing happiness of this life, yet it invariably eludes him. Give man everything he desires, and he will not be satisfied! His unhappiness may result from envy of others who have more of this world's goods than he has, or it may result from the fear of losing what has been accumulated. St. Augustine was right when he said to God: "Thou hast made us for Thyself, and our hearts cannot rest until they rest in Thee."

Death for the just means eternal life with God. Death for the just means freedom for both the body and the soul: for the body, freedom from pain and suffering, and for the soul, the intellect, illumined by the light of glory, a wisdom greater than all the sages of the world. And the will, perfected and confirmed in holiness by the Beatific Vision, will enable the saved to love fully and purely for eternity. In heaven, true happiness consists in possessing God utterly and seeing Him as He is. Small wonder Pope John XXIII could say: "Every day is a good day to be born; every day is a good day to die."

Conclusion

Let us pray earnestly at this funeral Mass that God, in His bountiful mercy, grant eternal life, liberty of the just, and eternal happiness to _____. An added charity would be to pray for the family that, by the grace of God, every member will come to accept this cross as a benevolent act of God's holy will. God's will is mercy itself.

TWENTY-FIRST HOMILY

General

Extension of sympathy to the family

Introduction

The great Jesuit saint, St. Aloysius Gonzaga, was born of a noble family near Mantua in 1568. While attending the sick during a plague, St. Aloysius contracted the disease and died at the age of thirty-one. In one of his last letters to his mother, whom he addressed tenderly as "most honored lady," the saint counseled her on how to react to the news of his approaching death. He begged her not to insult God's boundless loving kindness by mourning, as dead, one living face to face with God, one whose prayers could bring her more powerful aid than they ever could on earth. "Our parting," he wrote, "will not be for long; we shall see each other again in heaven and, together, enjoy eternal bliss." What an inspiring profession of faith!

Application

In the presence of the mortal remains of _____, it is not easy to suggest that, in reality, death is not something to be abhorred but, rather, something to be humbly accepted, since, as St. Aloysius could light-heartedly say to his revered mother: "Death is an invitation to eternal bliss with God in heaven." The Church echoes this same teaching in the Preface of this Mass, for the celebrant will say: "When the body of our dwelling lies in death, we gain an everlasting place in heaven."

We shall never understand death unless we reflect on the nature of the human soul; for man is composed of a material body and a spiritual soul, the latter made in the image and likeness of God, who is a pure spirit. Every living thing has within itself the source of its own activity. The source of activity in plants and animals is called the principle of life; in man, it is called the soul. The Council of Vienne (1312) declared that the rational soul is the life-giving principle of the human body.

We can learn something of man's soul by noting what it enables him to do. Each of the five senses of the body allows some knowledge to enter in, but only by things that are themselves material. For instance, we could never perceive the perfume of a rose unless the minute fragrant particles penetrate our nostrils. We could not really determine hardness or softness without touching some material things with those qualities.

But man knows more things than the five senses tell him. He can rise high above everything in the material, visible world. He can form ideas of "truth," "justice," "liberty," which are immaterial. He can think of God and angels, and he can love them; yet God and angels are pure spirits. It follows, then, that man's soul must be akin to them—therefore, immaterial, spiritual, and immortal. After death the soul can continue to exercise its higher spiritual activity, and it is this that should console the family and friends of _____.

While his (her) body will pay the common debt for the sin of Adam, his (her) soul, freed from this life, now exists apart from the body, and has gone on, we earnestly pray, into union with God in an eternity of bliss. On the last day, his (her) soul will be reunited to the mortal remains we reverently bless this day, for Scripture says: "The hour is coming when all those in their graves shall hear his voice and come forth. Those who have done right shall rise to life" (Jn. 5:28).

There are, as far as we know, but two glorified human bodies in heaven, the risen sacred body of our Redeemer, and that of his Immaculate Mother Mary. The mortal remains of all the other dead await the general resurrection on the last day. The saints we call upon to help us in our many needs are still buried on this earth. We can visit the tomb of St. Francis in Assisi, the tomb of the Little Flower in Lisieux, and that of St. Anthony in Padua. It is to the glorified souls of the saints in heaven that we address our prayers of petition and those of thanksgiving.

Conclusion

Since we find no difficulty in believing that the saints in heaven are alive, hear our prayers, interest themselves in our salvation, and secure favors for us from God while their sacred remains are still on this earth awaiting the resurrection, this should ease the burden on the family and relatives of _____. Keep in mind that all the faithful who have died in the state of grace are alive with God in heaven, or they are "saints in waiting" in purgatory, looking to us to speed their entrance into heaven by our Masses, Holy Communions, prayers, and almsgiving on their behalf.

My earnest prayer is that all of us will see in death what Father Lacordaire saw in it when he wrote: "If death is the masterpiece of divine justice, it is equally the masterpiece of God's love."

May all the faithful departed be numbered among the saints whose names are written in the Book of Life. Amen.

TWENTY-SECOND HOMILY

General

Extension of sympathy to the family

Introduction

It is said, according to Corbett, that over the triple doors to the great Cathedral of Milan there are three doorways spanning the arches. Over one is carved a beautiful wreath of roses, and underneath is the wording: "All that which pleases is but for the moment." Over another door is sculptured a cross, and underneath are inscribed these words: "All that troubles us is but for the moment." But over the great entrance to the center aisle is the inscription: "That only is important which is eternal."

Application

This is the message conveyed to us by the Son of God made Man when He posed the question: "What shall it profit a man if he gain the whole world and suffer the loss of his soul?" (Mk. 8:36–37) That question by our Lord has made many a person think of the importance of saving his or her immortal soul. St. Ignatius Loyola came upon that question of our Lord when he was convalescing from an illness; he was so moved by it that, right there and then, he resolved to abandon his military career to serve God in the religious life. Subsequently, St. Ignatius founded the Jesuits.

Since the salvation of one's immortal soul is of such great importance, I am confident that _____, who now knows more about the worth of the soul, its power, its greatness, would want me to use the occasion of his (her) funeral to enlighten all those present here this morning about the importance of saving their souls. Let us trace the history of a soul.

At the moment of conception, every individual soul is created out of nothing by God. On this, Pope Pius XII, in *Humani Generis*, teaches that "the Catholic faith obliges us to hold firmly that souls are immediately created by God." The soul is a spirit made in the image and likeness of God and infused into the body as its principle of life. "From the soul," says St. Augustine, "the body has feeling and life."

When God created Adam from the dust of the earth and "breathed into his face the breath of life, and man became a living soul" (Gen. 2:7), God endowed our first parents with wondrous gifts for soul and body: (1) sanctifying grace, which, as St. John Damascene asserts, "made them participants in his community"; (2) the gift of rectitude or integrity, which, as St. Augustine says, "made it possible for them to easily avoid sin"; (3) immortality for the body; (4) freedom from suffering; and (5) infused knowledge, natural knowledge suitable to their adult age and tasks, as well as a measure of supernatural knowledge which was necessary for them to reach their supernatural destiny.

When our first parents in Eden sinned grievously through their transgression of a divine command, their loss, and ours as well, was horrendous. Through their sin, our first parents lost sanctifying grace, being excluded thereby from friendship with God; and they became subject to sickness, pain, and death as punishment. This funeral today, as well as every funeral, is the result of Adam and Eve's sin.

Conclusion

Reflect now on how much God has valued each human soul since He sent His Divine Son to ransom us and open heaven to us. Jesus Christ, our Redeemer, became man and lived among us for thirty-three years and died on the cross to save us. Before His death, Christ instituted the seven sacraments, the most fundamental of which is baptism; by baptism, original sin and all other sins are cleansed from our soul; and through sanctifying grace we are made children of God, participants in His nature, and heirs to the kingdom of heaven. By the sacrament of penance we are freed from sins committed after baptism if we fulfill all the conditions for its worthy reception. The Sacrament of the Holy Eucharist has as its chief fruits: (1) intrinsic union with Christ; (2) it is a food for the soul, preserving and increasing the supernatural life of the soul; and (3) it is a pledge of heavenly bliss and of the resurrection of the body. The sacraments of holy orders and marriage confer sufficient grace for the recipients to fulfill the duties of their state in life. The sacrament of the sick, formerly called extreme unction, is a strikingly comforting sacrament for the aged, the sick, and the dying, as mentioned in St. James' Epistle (5:14–15). By the grace of the Holy Spirit, by the prayers and the anointings by the priest, sins are taken away, as well as the remnants of sins.

Let us raise our hearts in thanksgiving for all the gifts God has showered on _____'s soul and say: "May his (her) soul and the souls of all the faithful departed, through the mercy of God, rest in peace. Amen."

TWENTY-THIRD HOMILY

General

Extension of sympathy to the family

Introduction

On one occasion during the public life of our Blessed Lord, He took three of His disciples with Him to the top of Mount Tabor; and while there, He was transfigured before them. It was a most startling experience for the disciples. His divinity seemed to burst through His humanity as He prayed; "and his face became as dazzling as the sun, his clothes as radiant as light" (Matt. 17:2). At first the disciples, Peter, James, and John, were struck by the glory of the transfigured Christ, but their calm suddenly changed to terror, especially when "a bright cloud overshadowed them. Out from the cloud came a voice which said: 'This is my beloved Son on whom my favor rests. Listen to him.' When they heard this, the disciples fell forward on the ground, overcome by fear" (Matt. 17:5–6).

Application

That only three of the Apostles were privileged to witness the transfiguration causes some to feel that those who were on Mount Tabor were being prepared for the special roles they would be called upon to play, roles requiring strong faith and courage. St. Peter, for instance, would be called upon to head the Church after our Lord's ascension; St. James would be the first martyr among the Apostles; and St. John, the virgin Apostle, would be charged with the sublime task of writing the fourth Gospel and of being commissioned by our Holy Redeemer Himself from His cross on Calvary to take tender care of His sinless Mother Mary.

What St. Peter saw at the transfiguration on Mount Tabor influenced his whole life, and the memory of it stayed with him to the end of his life, for he made mention of the glory he had seen on Mount Tabor in his last inspired epistle before his own cruel martyrdom.

Let me mention another saint who had seen something of the glory of God. During the trial of St. Stephen, destined to be the first Christian martyr, he was "filled with the Holy Spirit, looked to the sky and saw the glory of God, and Jesus standing at God's right hand" (Acts 7:55). When the saint tried to tell the onlookers what he had seen, they dragged him out of the city and began to stone him. The saint could be heard to say in prayer: "Lord Jesus, receive my spirit." He fell to his knees, and cried out in a loud voice: "Lord, do not hold this sin against them." And with that he died (Acts 7:57–60). St. Stephen, having seen the glory of God and Jesus standing at God's right hand, deemed that no pain, no suffering was too high a price to pay for union with God.

One thing sustained _____ in his (her) final illness, and that was the hope of entering into a union with God where he (she) would be free from all evil and possess all good. To be free from all evil is basic to lasting happiness, yet, in this life, we are scarcely without the irksome struggle between body and soul. We have only to call to mind the passions that rage within us, and the anxiety and remorse that rack us. And how numerous are the ills to which the body is subject: accidents, chronic diseases, epidemics, and invalidism. Who would not reckon himself happy to be certain that never again for all eternity would he (she) know mental anguish or physical pain? Well, the good who die in the Lord are promised such a reward: "He shall wipe every tear from their eyes, and there shall be no more death or mourning, crying out or pain, for the former world has passed away" (Rev. 21:4).

Heaven is more than the absence of evil; it is the possession of all good. The essential glory of the saved consists in the Beatific Vision, whereby the blessed behold God face to face, love Him, and enjoy Him forever. It is the Beatific Vision which will satisfy all our faculties and constitute our consummate and unspeakable happiness; according to the words of Scripture, "You will show me the path to life, fullness of joys in your presence, the delights at your right hand forever" (Ps. 16:11).

Conclusion

Such is the happiness to which the love and mercy of God has called _____. Fortified as he (she) was by the sacrament of reconciliation, Viaticum (heavenly Food for the journey), the sacrament of the Sick, and the Apostolic Blessing, our firm hope is that he (she) is already enjoying the blissful banquet to which our Heavenly Father has called us all. If he (she) is detained in purgatory, the place of purification, this funeral Mass, your Communions, your prayers, and your alms will speed his (her) union with God. The Holy Souls in Purgatory are "saints in waiting."

May the family find comfort in these consoling words from Sacred Scripture: "Precious in the eyes of the LORD is the death of his faithful ones" (Ps. 116).

TWENTY-FOURTH HOMILY

For a young person

Extension of sympathy to the family

Introduction

G. F. Watts painted a famous work which he entitled "Happy Warrior." It is a picture of a young man snatched away in his prime. His country had called him to its service. He had no heart for war, but he was determined to be the best soldier he could be. He had gone out into combat with all his armor shining, and his eyes were bright with anticipation of victory. Almost in his first engagement he was struck down, paying the supreme sacrifice. The artist shows the helmit fallen back from the brave young face, as an angel bends over him and imprints the kiss of everlasting peace upon his brow.

Application

The Council Fathers of Vatican II remarked that the "mystery of death beggars the imagination," but never is death so mysterious as when it touches a young person. One of the things which many find hard to reconcile with the goodness of God is the death of a mere child or a young man or a young lady. When death comes to the aged, to those who have lived out their days, we come to accept it with a certain understanding and resignation, or, at least, with an absence of rebellion. But when the young are taken in the flower of their youth, it is most difficult to suppress the embittered protest, or staunch the burning tears.

To the bereaved family of _____, I may say that I am sure God understands your grief and tears. Our dear Lord Himself wept over the passing of a close family friend, Lazarus, brother of Martha and Mary. I recall reading that the great St. Bernard, in the throes of anguish at the death of his brother Gerard, prayed for his tears to flow in burning streams. He remarked that people told him not to weep, but he told them that he was not the type of person who was insensitive to the sorrows of death. "I feel it, I feel it," said St. Bernard, adding, "Let no person tell me that it is wrong to grieve over the loss of a loved one."

Care must be taken that grief does not take on the quality of rebellion or, worse, blasphemy. In a report of a frightful accident involving a school bus and the sad deaths of numerous children on their way to a holiday in France, a correspondent wrote of one mother who kept saying: "Where was God?" St. Paul tells us: "We would have you be clear about those who sleep in death, brothers; otherwise you might yield to grief, like those who have no hope. For if we believe that Jesus died and rose, God will bring forth with him from the dead those also who have fallen asleep believing in him" (1 Thess. 4:13–14). Note well that St. Paul does not say that we must not grieve—that would not be human: but he tells us not to grieve "like those who have no hope."

As Christian parents, relatives, and friends, we all must believe that _____ is alive, that his (her) life is not ended, but is merely changed. His (Her) soul (intellect, will, memory, even personality), now separated from the body, has not ceased to exist for an instant, nor will it ever cease to exist for all eternity.

Let us remember that the new life of the soul after death is not merely an extension of earthly life. The new life is the gift of God's creative power, a life wherein God will exert the powers of His omnipotence to make us supremely happy. In that everlasting life, our being will be gloriously expanded and our intelligence will be illumined by the light of glory, so that we shall be wiser than all the sages on the earth. Our will, too, will be transfixed, perfected, and confirmed in holiness forever by the Beatific Vision, so that we shall be unable to will the slightest thing apart from God's infinite good pleasure.

It is a defined doctrine of our holy faith that the dead, on the last day, will rise from the grave with the same bodies they had on earth. Every infirmity or physical imperfection of body or mind will have disappeared. St. Thomas speaks of the body rising in the "state of perfection."

Conclusion

So, dear parents, relatives, and friends, let us dry our tears and raise our hearts, for _____'s soul still lives and is, we hope and pray, with God in unbelievable happiness; the body we lay to rest today will rise to be reunited with the soul, and be spiritualized and glorified throughout all eternity. Let us here, today, so live as to assure ourselves union with _____ forever and ever. Keep in mind the words of Father Grasset: "Death is, for the saved, the kiss and consummation of love."

It was divine love that caused God to put _____ on this earth. It was love that moved Him to take him (her) to Himself. Happy is the family with some members in heaven to help those who are still here below!

TWENTY-FIFTH HOMILY

General

Extension of sympathy to the family

Introduction

Diodorus Siculus, a Greek historian who lived before the Christian era, writes that the Egyptians looked upon their homes as mere places of pilgrimage and their tombs as their permanent dwelling places. This sort of thinking may very well furnish a reason for the gigantic sepulchers built for their dead. Somehow, all the pagans had a vague idea of life after death, since tombs opened after thousands of years reveal food and grain buried with the dead.

Application

It must be said that the Chosen People themselves had a vague notion of the hereafter, although God protected them always from falling into the pagan errors of dualism and pantheism. While they believed in the other world, they gave more thought to national prosperity and personal happiness. It is true that they had a Hebrew word *Sheol* which in the Old Testament meant the "grave" or the "other world of good or evil." Job thought of *Sheol* as a gloomy place. How depressing were his comments:

> I should be as though I had never lived; I should have been taken from the womb to the grave. Are not the days of my life few? Let me alone that I may recover a little. Before I go whence I shall not return, to the land of darkness and of gloom, in the black, disordered land where the darkness is the only light (Job. 10:19–22).

After the Exile, the curtain was raised to afford rays of new light. The Book of Wisdom clearly expresses the idea of immortality:

> But the souls of the just are in the hand of God: and no torment shall touch them. They seemed, in the view of the foolish, to be dead; and their going away was thought an affliction, and their going away from us, utter destruction, but they are at peace. For if before men, indeed, they be punished, yet is their hope full of immortality (Wis. 3:1–4).

How direct and pointed is the resurrection professed:

> Many of those who sleep in the dust of the earth shall awake: some shall live forever, others shall be in everlasting horror and disgrace (Dan. 12:2).

In the New Testament, our Lord removed all doubt about life after death. Christ claimed that He was the "resurrection and the life," and proved it by restoring life to the dead. He held out the promise that He Himself would rise from the dead; this He did on the first Easter morning. To the Apostles, the resurrection of our Lord was the foundation on which the Church was built. In the resurrection of our Lord, the Apostles saw victory over death for all His followers. In the Creed attributed to them, do we not all say: "I believe . . . in the resurrection of the body and life everlasting"?

The day _____ was baptized, not only was the stain of original sin washed away, but he (she) became a child of God and an heir to the kingdom of heaven. Through the infusion of sanctifying grace he (she) was given a share in the Divine Life, and made a member of Christ's Mystical Body. According to St. Paul, in baptism, we were baptized into Christ's death and went into the tomb with him, only to rise to a new life (see Rom. 6:3–5). Baptism is a commitment to an abiding faith in Christ and His teachings!

When St. Paul spoke of baptism as related to Christ's death, burial, and resurrection to a new life, it was much more clearly understood by converts in the early days of the Church. Baptism at that time was by immersion. Being *immersed* beneath the water, they were thereby, as it were, buried with Christ, sharing His being dead to sin; and when the new Christians *emerged* from beneath the water, they thereby arose, as it were, with Christ from the tomb, sharing the new life of the Risen Lord.

At the funeral of a Catholic, the celebrant of the Mass meets the mortal remains at the door of the church and prays over the deceased person and sprinkles the casket with holy water. Following this, a white cloth or a pall is placed over the casket. The white cloth covering on the casket serves as a reminder of the white baptismal robe once worn by the deceased on the day of his (her) baptism.

Conclusion

My dear friends, _____ was baptized and began a new life which did not end the day he (she) died; rather, it will continue, we prayerfully hope, for all eternity in heaven. Oh, the consolation in these inspired words: "If we have died with Christ, we believe that we are also to live with him" (Rom. 6:8).

Our most earnest prayer at this Mass is that the moment of _____ _____'s death was the moment when God took him (her) into His fatherly arms, there to enjoy eternal beatitude.

In a collection of singular epitaphs, I found this one unique:

"Blessed be God who placed hope on the grave."

TWENTY-SIXTH HOMILY

General

Extension of sympathy to the family

Introduction

Benjamin Franklin wrote to a friend with whom he shared the loss of a mutual friend:

> We are spirits. That bodies should be lent to us, while they can afford us pleasure, assist us all in acquiring knowledge, or in doing good for our fellowmen, is a kind and benevolent act of God. When they become unfit for these purposes and answer none of the intentions for which they were created, it is equally kind and benevolent that a way is provided by which we may shed them. Death is that way. Our friend and we are called to a beatitude that will last forever. His conveyance was ready first, and he has gone on before us. We could not conveniently start together; but why should you and I grieve at this, since we are soon to follow, and know where to find him?

Application

Benjamin Franklin's observations on the death of his friend were well taken. He stressed the spirituality and immortality of the human soul, and considered death as a benevolence on the part of God, in as much as it freed the soul for more perfect union with God. Before Benjamin Franklin, St. Paul had written: "I long to be freed from this life and to be with Christ, for it is the far better thing" (Phil. 1:23). Admirable were Franklin's concept of the everlasting beatitude of heaven and his off-hand allusion to the certitude of his own death; as the Psalmist said: "What man shall live and not see death?" (Ps. 89:49) Franklin concluded his letter by counseling his friend not to grieve over the news of their mutual friend's death, but, rather, to envy him.

Today, no one questions the inevitability of death, yet our present society, secular and existential, offers little of the spiritual comfort that eased the passing of our ancestors from this life to the next. Dr. Herman Feifel, a psychologist with the Veterans Administration in Los Angeles, once remarked that death has been transformed from "a doorway to a wall," representing the ultimate personal disaster in a solipsistic age rather than a meaningful transition to something new and better.

To Christ, the Son of God made Man, death was not a wall, but a gateway to a new life. Did our Lord not say to Martha before raising her brother from the grave: "I am the resurrection and the life; he who believes in me, even if he die, will come to life"? (Jn. 11:26) Christ demanded an act of faith on the part of Martha to His question: "Do you believe this?" Her reply was: "Yes, Lord." It was on the strength of her answer that Christ proceeded to Lazarus' tomb.

The great St. Paul saw death as the gateway to a new life, or why would he have written: "If we have died with Christ, we believe that we are also to live with him"? (Rom. 6:8) St. Teresa of Avila, Doctor of the Church, boldly professed: "I cannot live without Christ; I will gladly die to see him." St. Francis of Assisi, on his deathbed, asked: "Brother physician, tell me without misgiving whether death is very near—it will be the gate of life for me." According to Thomas of Celano, present with St. Francis when he died, the last words of the Little Poor Man of Assisi, and of the world, were: "Welcome, Sister Death."

Sorrow must not blind the family of _____ today. Our faith must dominate our grief. His (Her) soul, we confidently hope, has gone into an eternity of bliss, or it soon will enter therein through this Mass, our Communions, prayers, and almsgiving. This mortal body, sacred to us because it was the tabernacle of his (her) soul, a soul wherein God Himself made His abode, this revered body which brought joy and comfort to the family, and which has paid his (her) part of the mortgage due to God by Adam's sin—this same body will rise from the grave on the last day, be reunited with his (her) soul already in heaven, and both will see God in heaven for an unimaginable ecstasy of eternal happiness. Our resolve today must be to do everything we must do to assure meeting him (her) in heaven.

While the pagans had a hazy concept of life after death, it never dawned on them that the body would rise from the grave and begin to live again. We do not have to guess about this; we know it for certain, for our Lord said: "No need for you to be surprised at this, for an hour is coming in which all those in their graves shall hear his voice and come forth" (Jn. 5:28).

Conclusion

The Gospel announces the death of God's own Divine Son in these simple words: "The hour had come for him to pass from this world to the Father" (Jn. 13:1). _____ passed from this world at God's own time. Using the words of Benjamin Franklin, I ask his question: "Why should you and I grieve at this, since we are soon to follow and know where to find him (her)?"

May the souls of the faithful departed rest in peace. Amen.

TWENTY-SEVENTH HOMILY

General

Extension of sympathy to the family

Introduction

It is related that Blessed Benincasa, a twenty-five-year-old member of the Servite Order, was granted permission to embrace the life of a hermit on a mountain near Siena. After a long life of prayer and penance he died alone, but his death was announced to the people living on the plains below by a very bright light streaming from the cave wherein he had lived and died.

Application

It is not by mere chance that two of the four Eucharistic Prayers used in the Mass commemorating the dead, plead for *light* for the deceased. Eucharistic Prayer Number I says: "May these, and all who sleep in Christ, find in your presence, *light*, happiness, and peace." Eucharistic Prayer Number II uses this petition: "Remember our brothers and sisters who have gone to their rest in hope of rising again; bring them and all the departed into the *light* of your presence." If a Communion hymn is not sung, then the celebrant of a second Mass on All Souls' Day will recite this Communion Antiphon:

> May eternal *light* shine on them, O Lord, with all your saints forever, for you are rich in mercy. Give them eternal rest, O Lord, and may perpetual *light* shine on them forever, for you are rich in mercy.

It was very early in the morning of the day our Lord came to the temple and began teaching the people during the feast of Tabernacles. This feast was one of the happiest of the Jewish calendar, and through the years it took on a carnival atmosphere. The people in the city evacuated their homes and built for themselves and their families lean-to's of branches and boughs to commemorate the hardships of the Chosen People during the forty years of their pilgrimage to the Promised Land. There was the usual procession to the temple with the container of water, calling to mind the miraculous passage of the Chosen People through the Red Sea. Once in the temple, there was the lighting of the great branch candelabra to commemorate the pillar of fire that guided the Chosen People each night of the forty years of the Exodus.

It may well have been the sight of the lighted candelabra, like tiny sparks in the massive temple, or the rising sun that crept into His Father's house, which, by full daylight, had gloriously lighted up the golden and marble magnificence of the temple, that moved Christ to proclaim: "I am the light of the world. No follower of mine shall ever walk in darkness; no, he shall possess the light of life" (Jn. 8:12).

The sunlight which flooded the temple and the court of the women where Christ proclaimed Himself the "light of the world" was the work of His creation. All the works of creation, including the sun, are works of the Three Divine Persons.* To be sure, the brightest sunshine is but a dim shadow of the glory and greatness of God. David could say: "O Lord, my God, you are great indeed! You are clothed with majesty and glory, robed in light as with a cloak" (Ps. 104:1–2).

Moses, descending from Mt. Sinai after receiving the Ten Commandments and other laws from God, while having only spoken to Him through a cloud during the span of forty days, found the skin of his face so brilliantly radiant that he had to cover his face with a veil (Exod. 34:30–35). When our Lord was transfigured on Mt. Tabor in the presence of Sts. Peter, James, and John, His divinity shone through His humanity: "his face became as dazzling as the sun, his clothes as radiant as *light*" (Matt. 17:2).

From the moment of _____'s baptism, the body we bless and honor today was a tabernacle for his (her) soul in which God made His abode. A soul in the state of grace is a thing of beauty in God's sight. St. Teresa of Avila said: "The beauty, glory, and light of a glorified soul is so great, that if we could see it, we would die of pleasure." Every sacrament worthily received by the deceased during his (her) life, increased the sanctifying grace received at baptism. The Holy Eucharist, for instance, was the Bread of Life for his (her) soul, was, as the Council of Trent taught, "a pledge of future glory and everlasting happiness."

Conclusion

Who among us could ever call the death of a true follower of Christ a tragedy? Death, for the person fortified for it by a worthy reception of the sacraments, transforms it into an instrument of triumph and victory. Think of the soul of _____ now caught up in the joy of seeing the infinite glory of God and being made welcome as an heir of God and His kingdom. There will be no other illumination in heaven but God Himself. "They will need no light from lamps or the sun, for the Lord God shall give them light, and they shall reign forever" (Rev. 22:5). And the body we lay to rest today shall rise from the dead, patterned on the risen, glorified Body of Christ, and filled with beauty and radiance. Keep these words in your heart, for Christ said: "The just shall shine as the sun in the kingdom of their Father" (Matt. 13:43).

Gentle Jesus, bring _____ into the light of your presence! Amen.

---

*The Council of Florence, 1441, so declared in the *Decretum pro Jacobitis*.

TWENTY-EIGHTH HOMILY

General

Extension of sympathy to the family

Introduction

Perhaps never before has the family of _____ been caught up so acutely in the need for a firm belief in a future life than it has during these last few days. How could it be otherwise? True, certain signs of approaching death have been evident in the past weeks (months), but, somehow, those near and dear to him (her) hoped that there would be a rally, a delay, or even a recovery. No matter how we are prepared for it, it is a shattering blow when death is officially pronounced. No other words are as devastating as those three words: "He (She) is gone!"

The only support available at such a time is our firm Catholic belief that, in death, life is changed, not ended. When the principle of life, the spiritual and immortal soul, takes leave of the body at the moment God calls it to Himself, the soul continues to go on living forever with God in the indescribable joy of heaven, if such a merciful reward has been merited. As to the body, because of the sin of Adam, it must remain behind until the last day, but it will rise from the dead in perfection and be glorious through reunion with the glorified soul.

Application

We have it on the word of Christ, the Son of God, that there is life after death. In His discourse to His Apostles at the Last Supper, Christ said:

> Do not let your hearts be troubled. Have faith in God and faith in me. In my Father's house there are many dwellings, otherwise how could I have told you that I am going to prepare a place for you? I am indeed going to prepare a place for you and then I shall come back and take you with me, that where I am you also may be (Jn. 14:1–3).

It would be quite understandable if the family members in the distress of these past days gave no specific thought to the words of the conclusion of the Apostles' Creed which have been said in our morning and/or evening prayers as a matter of custom: "I believe in the Holy Spirit, the Holy Catholic Church, the communion of saints, the forgiveness of sins, the resurrection of the body, and life everlasting." At this Mass, let us all renew that act of faith in the resurrection of _____ _____'s body, and his (her) everlasting life. These are words of truth and comfort.

The Fathers of Vatican Council II assert "that man is tormented not only by pain and the gradual breaking-up of the body, but also, even more, by the dread of forever ceasing to be. But a deep instinct leads him rightly to shrink from and to reject the utter ruin and total loss of his personality." Those of us in the household of the faith should give glory to God for the gift of being able to believe there is another and better life in the world to come.

We can feel for pagans who long for another life after this one, but who are void of certitude. Even Greek pagans, like Socrates, had a desire for a life after death, a life in which friendships would be continued. Before his judges, Socrates said:

> What a pleasure it will give to live with Palmeses and others, who suffered unjustly, and to compare my fate to theirs. What an inconceivable happiness will it be to converse with Sisyphus, Ulysses and others, especially as those who inhabit that world shall die no more.

Not only Greek philosophers, but Romans, such as Cicero, had similar ideas. Writing of the death of Cato, Cicero said:

> His soul, however, did not desert me, but still looked back on me in its flight to those happy mansions, to which he was assured I should one day follow him.

Sad, isn't it, that noted Greek and Roman pagan philosophers could only long for a place of happiness where they could meet their friends and continue their discussions in another life? The Fathers of Vatican Council II teach that the dread of forever ceasing to be is deeply instinctive in mankind, since man bears in himself the seed of eternity.

Happy for us that God in His goodness has given us the gift of faith and made us members of a Church, taught by divine revelation, that declares that God created man in view of a blessed destiny beyond the limits of his sad state on earth. God has called us to a life that is divine and free from all decay.

Conclusion

The pall of sadness that hangs over our hearts today should be lifted by the consideration of a doctrine of our holy faith: "that the souls of the just which in the moment of death are free from all guilt of sin, enter into heaven." Heaven is a place and condition of perfect supernatural bliss which consists in the immediate vision of God, and in the perfect love of God associated with it. We can hope that _____ _____ is with God and knows what St. Paul meant when he said: "No eye has seen, nor ear heard, nor the heart of man conceived, what God has prepared for those who love him" (I Cor. 2–9).

Eternal rest grant unto him (her), O Lord, and let perpetual light shine upon him (her)!

TWENTY-NINTH HOMILY

For an infant or a young child

Extension of sympathy to the family

Introduction

Surely the angels who stood guard over Christ's empty tomb could be excused for asking Mary Magdalene: "Woman, why are you weeping?" since no angels have ever known the agony of losing a relative or a close friend to death. Likewise, my attempts to assuage the tears, and bring consolation and comfort to the parents and family of little _____ _____, may be feeble indeed, for no one who has not experienced such a heavy cross can actually know the sorrow and pain of such a loss. All I can hope to do this morning is to set before you the example of a father, King David, of the Old Testament, who drank from the same cup the bitter dregs of the loss of a tiny infant son.

After a son had been born to Bethsheba, wife of Uriah and then of King David, the infant fell ill. The death of the child had been foretold by Nathan, the prophet, but David, nevertheless, besought God to spare the child. Scripture tells us:

> He [David] kept a fast, retiring for the night to lie on the ground clothed in sackcloth. The elders of his house stood beside him, urging him to rise from the ground; but he would not, nor would he take food with them. On the seventh day, the child died. David's servants, however, were afraid to tell him that the child was dead, for they said: When the child was alive, we spoke to him but he would not listen to what we said. How can we tell him the child is dead? He may do some harm! (2 Sam. 12:16–18)

When David noticed the servants whispering among themselves, he asked the question, the answer to which he feared so much: "Is the child dead?" They answered him: "Yes, he is dead."

Now, dear friends, listen to what followed:

> Rising from the ground, David washed and anointed himself, and changed his clothes, then he went to the house of the Lord and worshipped. He returned to his own house, where at his request food was set before him, and he ate. His servants said to him; 'What is this you are doing? While the child was living you fasted and wept and kept vigil; now that the child is dead, you rise and take food.' He replied: 'While the child was living I fasted and wept, thinking: "Perhaps the Lord will grant me the child's life. But now he is dead. Why should I fast? Can I bring him back again? I shall go to him, but he will not return to me" ' (2 Sam. 12:20–23).

Application

There are important lessons for all of us here this morning in the inspired Word of God relative to the passing of David's son. Let us reflect on what David did when the death of his son was confirmed. After making himself presentable, he went to the house of the Lord to worship the Creator of us all. This was David's way of submitting to the will of God. He needed strength in his hour of sorrow, and he sought solace in God's house. May I counsel the parents, family, and relatives to approach Christ in the Mass, in Holy Communion, in visits to the Blessed Sacrament; for our Lord Himself said: "Come to me, all you who are weary and find life burdensome, and I will refresh you" (Matt. 11:28).

Another point should be made here. In David's day, the full revelation of life after death and the glory of seeing God and being with him in heaven had not yet been unveiled clearly. They did conjecture that there was a place where the dead went. They called it *Sheol*, but Sheol was a dark and gloomy place. Even Sheol afforded David some comfort, for he could say: "I shall go to him, but he will not return to me."

Since the coming of Christ, we have the full revelation concerning life after death and the resurrection of the dead. Our Lord, by His cruel death and His resurrection from the dead, has conquered death. Before raising Lazarus from the dead, did Christ not proclaim: "I am the resurrection and the life: whoever believes in me, though he should die, will come to life"? (Jn. 11:26) At the Last Supper, our Lord told His Apostles that after His death He would rise from the grave and go to His Father to prepare a place for them, that where He was, they would be (Jn. 14:3). Oh, the comfort in Christ's words: "Father, I want those you have given me to be with me where I am so they may always see the glory you have given me" (Jn. 17:24).

Conclusion

The moment little _____ died, his (her) soul was in the presence of God. Baptism set him (her) apart to inherit the kingdom of God. Oh, the glory of it all! To enable his (her) intellect to see God, it was supernaturally perfected by *the light of glory*, as the Council of Vienne defined in 1311.

The mother of St. Maria Goretti was considered highly blessed and honored to be present for the canonization of her virginal daughter. Blessed, too, are you, the parents of little _____ , who was not old enough to offend God. Yes, blessed are you. You are the parents of a saint!

THIRTIETH HOMILY

General

Extension of sympathy to the family

Introduction

St. David the First, King of Scotland, was dying at Carlisle in 1153. St. Aelred, who was present, gives this account of his last hours:

> On the Friday he was anointed and given Viaticum, after which he spent time in reciting the Psalms with his attendants. On Saturday, they urged him to rest, but he replied: 'Let me rather think about the things of God, so my spirit may set out strengthened on its pilgrimage from exile to home,' and at dawn of Sunday, May 24, he passed away peacefully as if he slept.

Application

My dear friends, the exile of _____ has ended and he (she) has gone home. That life here on earth is merely a pilgrimage is not a concept of recent vintage, but goes back to Genesis, the first book of the Bible. When Jacob and his sons were presented to Pharaoh by his son Joseph, the king asked the patriarch how old he was, and he answered: "The years I have lived as a wayfarer amount to a hundred and thirty. Few and hard have been these years of my life, and they do not compare with the years that my ancestors lived as wayfarers" (Gen. 47:8–9).

St. Paul, in his Letter to the Hebrews, after defining faith "as the substance of things to be hoped for, the evidence of things that appear not," proceeds to cite examples of faith in some of the greats of the Old Testament, such as Abel, Enoch, Noah, Abraham, and Sara; and then he writes: "All of these died in faith. They did not obtain what has been promised, but saw and saluted it from afar. By acknowledging themselves to be strangers and pilgrims on the earth, they showed that they were seeking a homeland" (Heb. 11:13).

St. Peter was likewise inspired to write with manifest authority that this life on earth is in no way a lasting one, telling us: "Beloved, you are strangers and in exile" (1 Pet. 2:11). To the Old Testament patriarch Jacob, this life was but a place of pilgrimage leading to a higher and happier life. The Apostles Peter and Paul, who had the full revelation from Christ, considered this world as an inn, but not their true home. They considered themselves as pilgrims on this earth being tested and tried so as to merit the next life with God in heaven.

The Apostle of the Gentiles had pity for the faithful who set themselves on the things of this world rather than on the things of heaven. To such, St. Paul wrote: "As you well know, we have our citizenship in heaven; it is from there that we eagerly await the coming of our Savior, the Lord

Jesus Christ." As to the resurrection of the dead, he adds: "He [Christ] will give a new form to this lowly body of ours and remake it according to the pattern of his glorified body, by his power to subject everything to himself" (Phil. 3:20–21).

We are gathered here this morning for the funeral Mass for _____ _____, who has finished his (her) pilgrimage on this earth; and we trust that his (her) immortal soul, by the mercy of God, is with Him in heaven. Oh, what a pity that those of us here have not spent more time to explore what God has in store for those who serve Him faithfully in this life! In our childhood we learned that God made us to know, love, and serve Him in this life and to be happy with Him in the next. This whole life, then, is but a preparation for the next life with God in heaven. Here, we are but pilgrims.

The essential beatitude of heaven consists in the intuitive vision of God. The angels, the saints, and the saved participate in this vision which naturally belongs to God alone, by means of *the light of glory,* which is, according to Lessius, "a supreme irradiation and participation of that light by which God sees Himself, and by which the intellect is elevated to a Divine state."

While God is infinitely merciful, He is, at the same time, infinitely just; therefore, God's justice must be served. It is a solace to know that the Catholic Church, instructed by the Holy Spirit, has it from Holy Scripture and the ancient traditions of the Fathers that there is a place of purification called *purgatory,* where those who die in venial sins, or with temporal punishment still due from forgiven sins, go. We call the souls in purgatory "Holy Souls" who await entrance into heaven. They look to us to come to their assistance by our Masses said or heard, our Holy Communions, prayers, and almsgivings on their behalf. We loved them in life. Let us remember them in death.

Conclusion

Death for _____ was not a tragedy. It was a gain. It is a grace to see death as the gateway to eternal happiness. It is recorded that when St. Elizabeth of Hungary was dying, she turned her face to the wall and sang as if a nightingale were in her throat; she died singing in her ecstasy of love.

It is moving to read in Longfellow's *The Golden Legend* these consoling lines:

The grave itself is but a covered bridge
Leading from light to light, through a brief darkness.

May eternal light shine upon him (her). May he (she) rest in peace!

THIRTY-FIRST HOMILY

General

Extension of sympathy to the family

Introduction

My dear friends, we are gathered together in this church for what is one of the more difficult religious and social duties that the death of a member of a family, a relative, or a friend imposes upon us—participation in their funeral Mass. At a funeral we come face to face with the mystery of the Providence of God. The Church teaches that nothing happens in this world by pure chance or accident. Everything that happens is willed or permitted by God. We believe that God never makes a mistake, that He never does anything wrong, that all His works are righteous and all His ways are wise (Ps. 145:17). This teaching, all of us here must firmly hold. It brings comfort and strength.

It is said that Michelangelo, when he was well advanced in age, discussed with a close friend life and death, the successes and failures, the joys and sorrows of life here on earth. His friend remarked that, after all the joys and pleasures of life, it is hard to think of death. "Not at all!" replied Michelangelo. "Since life has been such a pleasure, death, coming from the same source, should in no way cause us anxiety or grief."

Application

It is painful to recall that our first parents disobeyed a direct command of their Creator, and in their failure, they opened a sluice gate that flooded this world with woe for themselves and all their descendants. They lost the friendship of God in losing sanctifying grace. Heaven was closed, and mankind lost its brilliance of intellect; and the human will was weakened, becoming thereby prone to evil. The human body lost its immunity to illness and disease, and incurred death. In their humiliating banishment from the Garden of Eden, Adam and Eve were given a ray of hope to sustain them, that God would send them a ransomer.

Through all the centuries of waiting for the ransomer, God made use of the Old Testament patriarchs and prophets to reveal the purpose of His will. Little by little, God prepared the Chosen People for the coming of the promised Messiah, by revealing to the prophets the place of His birth, His cruel passion and death in ransom for the sin of mankind.

Christ's divinity was revealed to His Mother Mary by an angel: "The Holy Spirit will come upon you, and the power of the Most High will overshadow you; hence, the holy offspring to be born will be called the Son of God" (Lk. 1:35). An angelic choir announced Christ's birth to

~~Son of God" (Lk. 1:35). An angelic choir announced Christ's birth to~~
the shepherds: "This day in David's city a savior has been born to you,
the Messiah and Lord" (Lk. 2:11).

Who could measure the love of God for fallen man, a love that would
send His own Divine Son to live as Man among us and die on a cross
in atonement for our sins? How incomprehensible is God's love!

During the three years of our Lord's public life on earth, He was
always burdened with the presence of death. At the pleading of a father
whose twelve-year-old daughter had died, Christ accompanied the distraught parent to his home, and there He restored the child's life. When
a close family friend, Lazurus, died and was buried, Christ wept at the
tomb, prayed to His Father, then raised him from the dead.

Another day, Christ and His disciples and the people who were following them were on their way to a town named Naim. As they approached the gate of the town, the group stopped to let a funeral procession pass by. Many people were in the cortege, since the funeral was
for a young man, the only son of his mother; and she was a widow. Our
Lord, seeing the bereaved mother, had compassion on her, and said to
her: "Do not cry." Then He stepped forward and touched the litter; at
this the bearers halted. Christ said: "Young man, I bid you get up."
The dead man sat up and began to speak. Then Jesus gave him back to
his mother (Lk. 7:13–15).

Holy Scripture tells us that it was "by the envy of the devil [that]
death entered the world" (Wis. 2:24). The same source tells us that the
devil tempted Eve to disobey God's command in the Garden of Eden,
that her fall and that of Adam brought about the closing of heaven and
the loss of bodily immortality for themselves and their descendants.
Christ came to reverse the devil's victory by dying on the cross and
rising from the grave. His resurrection was His promise of our resurrection from the dead: "I am the resurrection and the life; whoever
believes in me, though he should die, will come to life" (Jn. 11:26).

Conclusion

The gentle Christ who restored life to a twelve-year-old girl and to a
young man, the only son of a widowed mother, that same Christ is
present here in the tabernacle; and after the Consecration, He will be
present on the altar as a Victim, offering Himself to His Father, pleading
mercy for the deceased and strength for the bereaved family. Remember, Christ died and was buried, and thereby, conquered both death
and the grave for those who love Him. Believe it, _____
_____ will rise again!

THIRTY-SECOND HOMILY

General

Extension of sympathy to the family

Introduction

Dear friends, as far as we know, our Blessed Lord raised three persons from the dead during the three years of His public life. There was the raising to life of the young daughter of Jairus, of the widow's only son at Naim, of Lazarus, a close family friend of our Lord, at Bethany. It is also worthy of note that those raised from the dead fell into three age brackets: Jairus' daughter was a twelve-year-old child; the widow's only son who died in Naim was a mere youth. Did not our Lord address him as "young man" when He halted the pallbearers? As to Lazarus, it would seem that he was a mature adult.

It is also worthy of note that the miracles Christ performed in raising the dead to life were witnessed by large crowds. In recording the raising of Jairus' little daughter, St. Mark states that there was the noise "of people wailing and crying loudly on all sides" (Mk. 5:38). Holy Scripture records that when our Lord and His disciples were making their way to Naim, they were followed by a crowd. Nearing the gate of the town, a funeral procession approached from the opposite direction. The circumstances of the funeral were sad, indeed, since the dead youth was the only son of his mother; and she was a widow. It was for that reason "that a considerable crowd of townsfolk were with her" (Lk. 7:12). As for the raising of Lazarus, again the miracle took place in the presence of a crowd: "Many Jewish people had come out to console Martha and Mary over their brother" (Jn. 11:19).

Application

By raising those three persons from the dead, our Lord wished to confirm the faith of His disciples, as well as the faith of the large number of witnesses present at the miracles, that He was the long-promised Messiah, the Son of God, with power over life and death. For instance, while the stone was being removed from Lazarus' tomb, Christ lifted up His eyes to heaven and said: "Father, I thank you for having heard me. I know you always hear me, but I have said this for the sake of the crowd, that they may believe that you sent me" (Jn. 11:42).

Astounding as were the miracles just mentioned, our Lord had another miracle to perform that would prove beyond doubt that He was the Messiah, the Divine Son of God; He would suffer a cruel death on the cross and rise from the dead as a pledge of man's resurrection. Christ predicted His passion, death, and resurrection to His disciples: "When they met again in Galilee, Jesus said to them, 'The Son of Man is going to be delivered into the hands of men who will put him to death, and he will be raised up on the third day' " (Matt. 17:21–22). Christ offered His death to His Father in atonement for the sins of mankind; and since Christ was God, that atonement was infinite. Christ's resurrection from the dead was a promise of our resurrection as well. St. Paul writes: "Death came by a man [Adam]; hence the resurrection of the dead comes through a Man [Christ] also. Just as in Adam all die, so in Christ all will come to life again" (1 Cor. 15:21–22). It is this teaching that eases the deep pain of such a day as this.

In spite of the deep sadness of this day for the family of _____ _____, Holy Mother Church is making use of symbols rather than words to lift up our hearts. What she is doing is trying to give this funeral Mass the atmosphere of an Easter celebration. The priestly vestments are white, as they are on every Easter Sunday; there is a white pall covering the casket, reminiscent of the white garment used in the rite of baptism, the sacrament that made _____ a child of God and heir to the kingdom of heaven. Even the Paschal Candle is burning brightly, as it did last Easter, representing the Risen Christ. The blood-red nails represent the five wounds our Lord suffered as our Redeemer, so that by His death heaven would be open to us. The symbols of Easter remind us of Christ's glorious resurrection from the dead, and they remind us of our own resurrection from the dead on the last day.

Conclusion

After the words of Consecration at this funeral Mass for _____ _____, the same Christ who suffered and died on the cross, who was buried, and then arose from the grave, will be offering Himself as a Victim to His Father on behalf of _____, reconciling him (her) with his (her) Creator. In every Mass, we proclaim Christ's death, and His death is victory.

If _____ could speak to us this morning, I think he (she) would say what St. Ephrem said: "I call for the prayers of all those who have known me, of all those who have loved me."

Let us promise him (her) our prayers!

THIRTY-THIRD HOMILY

General

Extension of sympathy to the family

Introduction

When someone asked Cardinal Wiseman on his deathbed how he felt, he replied: "I feel like a schoolboy who has learned his lessons, and is now going home for his holidays." What a grace and blessing for anyone facing death, to look forward to it with such noble composure.

No other age has been as death-conscious as is ours. Ever since Dr. Elizabeth Kubler-Ross's book entitled *On Death and Dying* was published in 1969, a work that has sold perhaps a million or more copies, one book after another has hit the market; and the end is not in sight. Believe it or not, dozens of books on death for children have been published.

Application

In a world shaken loose from religion and being moored to existentialism and unadulterated secularism, mankind is striving to find a reason for life and death. The teachings of our holy faith on life and death are based on Scripture and Tradition. In capsulated form, the catechism tells us that God is the Supreme Being, an infinitely perfect spirit with understanding and free will, Creator and Lord of heaven and earth, and all things visible and invisible. God needed nothing to add to His happiness, but, wanting to share His happiness with others, He created spiritual beings having understanding and free will: these we call angels. The angels were tested to prove them worthy of heaven. Many failed and were punished. The good angels entered heaven to adore, love, and serve God, and protect us here on earth.

God created man, a combination of a physical, material body made from the dust of the earth, and created for him a spiritual soul made to His image and likeness, with understanding and free will. Our first parents were created in a state of sanctity and immortality. Man was created to know, love, and serve God in this life and to be happy with Him in heaven forever.

Adam and Eve failed the test God used to prove their fidelity to His law. They listened to one of the fallen angels, the devil, who came to them as a serpent; and Eve took fruit from the one tree in the Garden of Eden they were forbidden to touch. Adam also ate the forbidden fruit; the punishment was swift. Our first parents were banished from Paradise, and they and their decendants became subject to pain, disease, and death. Their understanding was darkened, and their will to do good was weakened. Worst of all, they lost God's grace and, on this account, all right to heaven. Heaven was closed. In love and pity, God consoled our first parents with the promise of a Messiah or Savior.

With the fall of man, one of the greatest love stories this world would ever see began to unfold. Having promised Adam and Eve that they could hope for a savior, God made the Jews His Chosen People. He gave His law to Moses; and through the centuries, He sent patriarchs, prophets, judges, and kings, to keep the promise He made to Adam and Eve alive. And God established a priesthood to offer worship by sacrifices that would prefigure the great sacrifice that would fulfill His promise to send a savior.

In God's own time, He sent His own beloved Divine Son to take flesh from the Virgin Mary through the overshadowing of the Holy Spirit; and the Child born of the Virgin Mother in Bethlehem was both God and Man; and His name is Jesus Christ. The angels who announced His birth to the shepherds called the Infant Jesus "a savior" and "the Messiah and Lord" (Lk. 2:11). Our Lord lived thirty-three years on this earth, preached the Good News, performed miracles to prove His divinity, chose the Twelve Apostles, instituted the seven sacraments and the Mass, was crucified for saying He was the Son of God. Christ died a cruel death, was buried, and arose from the grave on the third day, as He said he would. His death ransomed mankind by shedding His Precious Blood; God's friendship was restored and heaven opened. Christ's resurrection was a pledge of our resurrection from the grave. When He ascended into heaven, Christ promised that He was going to make a place for us with Him, if we merit such a reward.

Conclusion

My friends, today we are in the presence of death. Never let us consider death as an injustice. St. Ambrose says that God did not decree death from the beginning; He prescribed it after the sin of our first parents as a remedy. It was by the death of our Lord that the world was redeemed. Christ did not seek to escape it, nor did His sinless Mother Mary. Both died and were buried.

In this funeral Mass for the repose of the soul of _____ _____, Christ, who died on the cross, will be on the altar after the Consecration, to renew the Sacrifice He offered on Calvary, for the repose of the faithful departed, and for us, the living. Let us pray for the grace of a happy death. It is said that when Pope John XXIII was dying, he said:"My bags are packed; I am ready to go." May we all be ready to say that when our time comes!

THIRTY-FOURTH HOMILY

General

Extension of sympathy to the family

Introduction

There is something extraordinary about the English martyrs in that, in nearly every instance, no matter how repulsive the form of the execution, death for them was an adventure. A case in point was the death by hanging of the secular priest Blessed Thomas Tunstal in 1616, at Norwich jail. For some reason, there was a considerable delay in the carrying out of the sentence. Blessed Thomas asked what time it was; when he was told it was eleven o'clock, he said: "Then it is near lunchtime"; and he uttered this prayer: "Sweet Jesus, admit me, though most unworthy, to be a guest this day at your table in heaven." He blessed the rope and the executioner, and said: "Jesus, have mercy on me!" and was dispatched into eternity to win a martyr's crown from the King of Martyrs, Christ the Lord.

Application

Generally, men fear death because they have never considered the purpose of life itself. It is of prime importance for us to acknowledge that God made each one of us, body and soul, and thus we are His creatures and must fulfill the end of our creation, which is the glory of God: "The Lord has made everything for his own ends" (Prov. 16:4). While everything God created, animate and inanimate, was made for His glory, in giving man intellect and free will He requires of him a special glory. Man gives this glory by knowing, loving, and serving God in this life, the reward for which is eternal happiness with God in the next life. The point is that we must keep ever before us the fact that man is chiefly for the life beyond the grave. In this life we are pilgrims, or, as St. Paul says, ". . . we have here no lasting city, we are seeking one which is to come" (Heb. 13:14).

It is an immutable law of God that all must earn or merit heaven. We merit heaven by striving to know God by means of faith in the truths Christ has revealed to us. We must fulfill the will of God by keeping His commandments: "If you wish to enter into life, keep the commandments" (Matt. 19:17). Finally, we must avail ourselves of the means of grace, of which the chief ones are Holy Mass, the sacraments, and prayer.

Created, as we all have been, for eternal happiness with God in heaven, why then should we consider death such a terrible tragedy? Scripture assures us that none can "avoid coming to the grave" (Ps. 49). St. Ambrose tells us that Christ did not need to die if He did not want to, but He did not look on death as something to be despised, something to be avoided; for the Son of God did not think it beneath His dignity, nor did He seek to escape it. Death is really the gate through which all of us must pass to reach heaven.

Why, then, do we fear death so much? A God who loved us enough to want to share heaven with us, a God who loved us enough to send His own Divine Son to redeem us by His death on the cross, surely would not abandon us in the crucial passing from this life to the next? Is it the fear of pain involved in dying? Pain anticipated is scarcely as bad as we imagined. We know this from our dread of a dentist's office, or surgery in a hospital. Whatever distress is involved in dying, if such sufferings are united to the sufferings of Christ, they are highly meritorious. St. Peter says: "Rejoice instead, in the measure that you share Christ's sufferings. When his glory is revealed, you will rejoice exultantly" (1 Pet. 4:13).

It just may be that there is a certain sweetness in dying that escapes us. Suarez, the great theologian whose teachings fill many volumes, exclaimed on his deathbed: "I never thought it was so sweet to die." Given such a gift of jubilee, St. Mary d'Oignies sang or recited verses for three days and nights before she died. St. Francis of Assisi, when told the end was approaching, said: "How welcome and beloved are you, my Sister Death!"

Conclusion

Those left behind should remember that gracious promise from the lips of Christ and be consoled by it, for our Lord said: "This is the will of him who sent me: that I should lose nothing of what he has given me; rather that I should raise it up on the last day" (Jn. 6:39). What a glorious promise, a promise of the resurrection of the mortal remains of _____ on the last day. Meantime, his (her) immortal soul has gone to be with God in the bliss of eternal joy. At the end of the world the body we honor and bless today will rise from the grave to be reunited to his (her) soul, and both will enjoy the vision and glory of the Triune God for ever. _____, Christ is yours; heaven is yours; rise and live for ever. Amen.

THIRTY-FIFTH HOMILY

General

Extension of sympathy to the family

Introduction

While St. Flavian was awaiting execution in the year 250, his mother urged him to glorify God by dying a martyr's death. The night before his beheading he saw, in vision, St. Cyprian, who was himself a martyr. Being asked whether the death stroke was painful beyond endurance, St. Cyprian replied: "The body feels no pain when the soul gives itself entirely to God. Trust the infinite power and wisdom of God."

Application

St. Paul was the only Apostle who had not known Christ in His earthly life. Saul is the name Paul was known by, prior to his conversion. He had gained the reputation of being a fierce zealot for the Jewish faith and a persecutor of the followers of Christ. He was greatly feared by the early Christians; in fact, he was on his way to Damascus to arrest some Christian men and women when, by the grace of God, his marvelous conversion took place. The power, the wisdom, and the infinite love surrounding his conversion on the road to Damascus never left his mind.

The power of God was evidenced to him by the brilliant light that surrounded him as he fell to the ground, and the awesome authority of the Voice that questioned him: "Saul, Saul, why do you persecute me?" "Who are you, sir?" he asked. The Voice answered: "I am Jesus, the one you are persecuting." Finally, instantaneous and total blindness befell him. The wisdom of Christ was made evident by His calling Saul by name, by His knowing where Judas lived on Straight Street in Damascus, and again by His knowing what Saul would be doing when Ananias, whom He was sending, would get there. Saul would be praying (Acts 9:12). The mercy of God was made evident by the salutation of Ananias, who addressed him as "Brother Saul"; and when the disciple said that the Lord Jesus had sent him, he was informed that he would receive the Holy Spirit and that his sight would be restored. Immediately, something like scales fell from his eyes and he regained his sight. Saul got up and was baptized.

Saul, the persecutor of Christians, now by the grace of God changed in name and heart to Paul, the Apostle, had a consuming desire to know Christ and the power of His resurrection. In his Epistle to the Philippians, St. Paul wrote; "I wish to know Christ and the power flowing from his resurrection; likewise to know how to share in his sufferings by being formed into the pattern of his death. Thus do I hope that I may arrive at resurrection from the dead" (Phil. 3:10–11). You see, Saint Paul was the kind of person who was not satisfied knowing a truth unless he also knew its power; unless, that is, he felt its influence upon himself.

The resurrection of our Lord from the dead was the foundation of his faith, as it should be of ours. In writing to the Corinthians, St. Paul recalls to them "how Christ died for our sins in accordance with the Scriptures: that he was buried and, in accordance with the Scriptures, rose again on the third day . . . If there is no resurrection of the dead, Christ himself has not been raised, and if Christ has not been raised, our preaching is void of content and your faith is empty too" (1 Cor. 15:12–18).

Whenever we proclaim, "Christ is risen," hidden under that act of faith is the truth that we too shall rise again. But St. Paul was moved to scrutinize the power of Christ's resurrection because he felt that it should work some powerful change in and on him. It was not simply that, by Christ's death and resurrection, the life we now live here on earth would be stretched out into eternity and never end. There are many people who would not consider such a thing to be a great boon. It was St. Paul's teaching that the quality of life would be changed. Writing to the Romans, he said: "As Christ was raised from the dead by the glory of the Father, we too will live a new life" (Rom. 6:5). *There* is the power of the resurrection—a new life in the kingdom of heaven.

Conclusion

My dear friends, a firm belief that _____'s life is not ended, but simply changed, must, of necessity, afford comfort to the family. Likewise, the teaching of the Church that Christ's resurrection from the dead is a pledge that _____, too, will rise from the grave on the last day, must assuage our grief. His (Her) soul, we can hope and pray, is with God in the new life St. Paul mentioned. At the end of the world, his (her) soul and body will be reunited, to walk in the newness of life in the ultimate joy of possessing God for all eternity.

Is it any wonder that Holy Scripture says: "Better the day of death than the day of birth"? (Eccl. 7:1)

THIRTY-SIXTH HOMILY

General

Extension of sympathy to the family

Introduction

St. Clare endured years of illness before the final agony set in, in 1253, lasting seventeen days. Her sister, St. Agnes, and the community surrounded her deathbed when they heard her say to herself: "Go forth in peace, for you have followed the good road. Go forth without fear, for He who created you has always protected you and loves you as a mother. Blessed be you, O God, for having created me." Shortly after, her saintly soul went forth to God.

Application

All one has to do is to think of all that God has done for _____ _____ to move us to offer profound adoration and thanksgiving to God even on this sad day in our lives. Consider that there was a time when he (she) did not exist. Suppose ten years before his (her) birth someone had walked down his (her) street and asked for him (her) by name, no one, not even the persons who were to become his (her) parents, would have known him (her).

In God's own time, he called him (her) into being and created for him (her) a spiritual soul made in His own image and likeness. Let us consider the ways a human soul images God: (1) God is a Spirit (Jn. 4:25), and the human soul is spiritual. (2) There are three Persons in God, and the human soul has three faculties: intellect, will, and memory. (3) God had no beginning and will have no end. The human soul had a beginning, but it will never cease to live. It is immortal.

Giving life to _____ was but the start of God's benefactions. Through a providential design, he (her) was born into a Catholic family, thus assuring him (her) instruction in the faith and good parental example. Shortly after birth he (she) was baptized, and a whole series of wondrous events resulted therefrom. His (Her) soul was cleansed of original sin through the infusion of sanctifying grace; this made him (her) an adopted child of God, able to call God "Father," call Christ, "Lord" and "Savior," and be a tabernacle of the Holy Spirit. Through baptism, he (she) was given a share in the Divine Life, made a member of Christ's Mystical Body, and heir to the kingdom of heaven.

At the moment of baptism, other great heavenly gifts were bestowed by God. Three great virtues or powers were infused by the Holy Spirit into his (her) soul, namely, faith, hope and charity, virtues that unite the soul to God. The effect of faith was to help him (her) to believe firmly in the existence of God and in His perfections. Hope aided him (her) to look for eternal salvation, and the means to attain it. The virtue of charity aided him (her) to find great satisfaction in God, and an abundant love to seek to please Him by keeping the commandments.

Gift followed gift. For instance, the cardinal virtues of prudence, justice, temperance, and fortitude were sown in his (her) soul, along with the moral virtues of humility, obedience, meekness, liberality, temperance, chastity, and diligence in doing what is good.

There seems to have been no end to God's gifts to _____ _____. Like a great monarch with a magnificent court, sanctifying grace, infused at baptism, brought him (her) seven more spiritual gifts, the gifts of the Holy Spirit. These gifts were wisdom, understanding, knowledge, counsel, fortitude, piety, and the fear of the Lord. The first four enlighten the understanding; the others strengthen the will. Confirmation increased those gifts.

All the other sacraments worthily received during his (her) life increased sanctifying grace given in baptism. Penance removed sins committed after baptism; and Holy Communion was food for the soul, bearing the seeds of resurrection unto life everlasting. The sacrament of the last anointing brought forgiveness; Viaticum brought food for the journey; and the giving by the priest of the Apostolic Blessing removed any obstacles to prompt union of the soul with God in heaven. Tell me, I beg you, what more could God have done for the salvation of _____ _____'s immortal soul? What God has done for him (her), He is doing for us. Let us thank Him at this Mass.

Conclusion

This funeral will be itself a great sermon to us all if we learn from it, first, God's love for us in that He sent His own Son to die for us; secondly, that Christ made Man will be a victim on the altar after the Consecration to renew and continue the Sacrifice of Calvary for the deceased and for us; finally, that we are only pilgrims and exiles in this life, being tested for eternal life with God.

As we leave the church, let us hear Christ say: "What profit does a man show who gains the whole world and destroys himself in the process?" (Mk. 8:30). That question has saved countless souls!

May the souls of the faithful departed rest in peace. Amen.

THIRTY-SEVENTH HOMILY

General

Extension of sympathy to the family

Introduction

Even when death strikes a close relative or friend, we somehow fail to think of it as a universal law for all mankind. The loss is so painful and so personal that we feel singled out to bear this cross alone; yet we are not alone. I read recently that nearly 4,800 burials take place each year in St. Raymond's Cemetery, the Bronx, one of the largest Catholic burial sites in New York. Every funeral we attend, every cemetery we pass, should remind us that we are pilgrims on this earth and that we do not have here a lasting city. We have been placed on this earth to know, love, and serve God in this life and to be happy with Him in the next life.

It is estimated that there are more than three billion people in the world today. In fifty years most of those will have died. In a hundred years, only a few will be left, and those will be living from day to day on borrowed time. Death is an inescapable experience, for St. Paul writes: ". . . it is appointed that men die once, and after death be judged" (Heb. 9:27).

Application

The Council Fathers of Vatican II, in the decree *The Church Today*, stated that man was created by God for a blissful purpose beyond the reach of earthly misery, that death is the result of Adam's sin, and that Christ, the Son of God, by His cruel death on the cross has restored us to wholeness. The Council Fathers were but stating the traditional teaching of the Church: (1) that man was created to be with God in an eternity of bliss; (2) that death is the result of Adam's sin; and (3) that God has called man and still calls him to cleave with all his being to Him in sharing forever a life that is divine and free from all decay. Christ won this victory when He rose to life, for by His death He freed man from death (1 Cor. 15:56–57).

It is very moving to consider that God needed nothing to add to His happiness; yet in His infinite goodness, He made angels and mankind, so they might share His happiness. St. Gregory Nazianzen was of the opinion that God did not desire a happy solitude or a lonely beatitude. God could have created the angels and man without free will, but He preferred to leave them free to choose or reject Him. How else could their love be tested and proved? Pride, Scripture tells us, caused many of the angels to fall from grace; and their loss was eternal. The faithful angels enjoy eternal bliss.

The test for man concerned obedience. Our first parents were placed in the Garden of Eden with everything essential for their needs. God made trees grow that were delightful to look at and good for food, with the tree of life in the middle of the garden and the tree of the knowledge of good and bad. Adam and Eve were told by God that they were free to eat from any tree in the garden except the tree of knowledge of good and evil. "From that tree you shall not eat; the moment you eat from it you are surely doomed to die" (Gen. 2:16–17). Tricked by the devil, Adam and Eve put their wills above that of God, their Creator. Their sin closed heaven to themselves and to their descendants. They were banished from the Garden of Eden and condemned to earn their food by the sweat of their brow; and death became man's inevitable lot.

An infinitely merciful God would not abandon His children; He sent His own Divine Son who took on our human nature to suffer and die on the cross to ransom us. His death opened heaven, conquered death; and His resurrection from the dead is a pledge of our resurrection on the last day.

Conclusion

_____'s soul, we can hope, has gone into eternity with God. Not for one instant has his (her) soul ceased to live. We may find it difficult to think of life outside the body. The angels are pure spirits, and they exist without material bodies. The souls of the saints are with God in heaven, and we pray to them for help; nevertheless, their bodies are still in this world awaiting the general resurrection. The immortal soul of _____ lives on.

I have a feeling that the loneliest funeral this world has ever seen, occurred when Adam and Eve buried their son outside Eden, a son slain by his own brother. Having cut themselves off from God by the original sin, they had no one to turn to for help. Surely, they agonized over the thought that they too would have to die, and all their descendants after them. I think they wept copious tears for their dead son Abel that day, and I think they wept tears for you, dear parents, relatives, and friends here this morning, and, indeed, for everyone who ever has or will shed a tear over the passing of a loved one.

O God, give him (her) a safe lodging, a holy rest, and peace!

THIRTY-EIGHTH HOMILY

General

Extension of sympathy to the family

Introduction

When St. Agnes of Montepulciano, one of the great saints of the Order of Preachers, was on her deathbed, she tried to stem the tears of the nuns gathered around her. Smiling, she said: "If you loved me, you would be glad because I am about to enter the glory of my Spouse. I shall not lose sight of you, and you will possess me forever." The gentle saint was forty-nine when she died.

Application

Blessed is the man or woman who can come to the end of this earthly pilgrimage and have the faith that banishes fear, and the hope that God, who has continuously showered good things on them during life, will not terminate His benefactions on their deathbed. "The just man," wrote Bossuet, "regards death as the moment when God will take him down from the cross, and receive him into His fatherly arms, there to enjoy eternal beatitude."

Why, then, do we weep over those who have gone on before us to the throne of God? Would we ask our dead to surrender the present peace, happiness, rest, or love they now experience in their new existence? What may baffle us is that the soul which we have never seen still lives, and the body, separated from it, must be laid to rest in the earth from which it was made, remaining there under the watchful eye of its Creator until the resurrection of all the dead at the end of the world.

Let us face it. Is it not we, who have suffered the loss of a loved one, who are victims of a sort of selfishness? Death surely creates a void in our lives. A cherished member of the family is taken from us, and part of us dies. God, in His wisdom, foresaw that there would be such occasions in our lives when we would need a release from such great tensions, and that tears would be a release-valve. From the first funeral, at which Adam and Eve wept bitter tears over their murdered son's grave, to this funeral, and to all that will follow to the end of time, tears will embalm the dead.

The very Son of God, our Lord Jesus, wept at the grave of a friend, as recorded in a very short inspired sentence in St. John's Gospel: "And Jesus wept" (Jn. 11:35). Christ was truly Man as well as God. As Man, Christ experienced all the human emotions, such as joy and grief, betrayal by friends, everything except sin. Christ gave proof of His humanity, in that, as Man, He *could* weep; and as a merciful Man, He *would* weep before He gave proof of His divinity by restoring life to the dead and buried Lazarus.

Our tears over the loss of a dear one Christ understands. What He won't understand is a grief that stifles and destroys. A river keeping within the bounds of its banks is something beneficial, but let floods come to destroy the banks of the river, and you have disaster. There is no fault in weeping over the loss of a loved one, for not every display of sorrow is a sign of a lack of trust in the providence of God. Natural grief is one thing, but sorrow that stems from lack of hope is quite another thing. That sorrow or grief which flows from rebellion against God's holy will, that grief that cuts one off from the needs of the other members of the family, or our neighbors, is a destructive sorrow unbecoming a true follower of Christ.

Conclusion

The death of a loved one, or even our own death, would not dismay us if we would keep in mind that we are all living in this world as exiles and aliens. This world is not a permanent home for any of us. When the day of our homecoming puts an end to our exile by freeing us from the bonds of this world, we are restored to paradise; and this we should welcome.

What person stationed in a foreign land would not want to return to his country as soon as possible? Well, we look upon heaven as our true country, and we long to see God in all His glory. There are in heaven generations of relatives who await us. Assured though they are of their own salvation, they are still concerned about ours. Oh, the delight of that heavenly kingdom where there is no more fear of death! Oh, the supreme and endless bliss of everlasting life!

Dear relatives and friends of _____, let us thank God for all the good things He has showered on him (her) during his (her) life on earth. May all the good he (she) has done on earth be turned into heavenly treasure.

Let us say to _____ these moving lines of Alexander Pope:

Take these tears, mortality's relief,
And 'til we share your joys, forgive our grief.

THIRTY-NINTH HOMILY

General

Extension of sympathy to the family

Introduction

A Greek by the name of Aristeides, who lived in the year 125 A.D., wrote to one of his friends about something that seemed strange to him about Christians; this is what he said: "If any religious person among the Christians passes away from this world, they rejoice and offer thanks to their God, and they escort the body with songs and thanksgiving, as if the dead person was setting out from one place to another nearby."

Application

Dear friends, here we are today, over two thousand years later, attending the funeral of a righteous Christian, and the liturgical formula of this Holy Sacrifice of the Mass is anything but morbid. The prayers offered are ones of hope in an eternity of everlasting bliss. The Scriptural readings confirm the sure basis for such hope. The Preface of this Mass directs that "when the body of our earthly dwelling lies in death, we gain an everlasting place in heaven."

The late Pope Paul VI, of happy memory, in his *Credo of the People of God*, again reaffirmed the consoling doctrine of the Communion of Saints when he said: "The communion of all the faithful of Christ; those who are pilgrims on earth; the dead who are attaining their purification, and the blessed in heaven, all together form one Church; and we believe that in this communion the merciful love of God and His saints is ever listening to our prayers, as Christ told us: 'Ask and you will receive.' Thus, it is with faith and hope that we look forward to the resurrection of the dead, and life in the world to come."

Brilliant and practical, St. John Chrysostom defined death as "the separation of the soul from the body." "For with the soul departing," continued St. John Chrysostom, "the soul lives forever and knows no death because it is from the breath of God; only the body dies, for there is that in us which is mortal and that which is immortal." The basis for such a belief in the immortality of the soul is founded on the word of the Son of God Himself. He said: "I am the resurrection and the life: whoever believes in me, though he should die, will come to life; and whoever is alive and believes in me will never die" (Jn. 11:26). As to the resurrection from the dead, did our Lord not say: ". . . no need to be surprised at this, for an hour is coming in which all those in their tombs shall hear his voice and come forth" (Jn. 5:28)?

It was on the basis of deep and abiding faith in Christ's own words that St. Paul reproached those whose sorrow over the loss of a loved one is prolonged and excessive. Writing to the Thessalonians, the Apostle said: "We would have you be clear about those who sleep in death, brothers; otherwise you might yield to grief, like those who have no hope. For if we believe that Jesus died and rose, God will bring forth with him from the dead those also who have fallen asleep believing in him" (1 Thess. 4:13–14).

St. Paul's teaching should impress all of us here this morning, since, if we believe in Christ, we must have faith in His words and promises. Each one of us here must realize that we are living as exiles and aliens in this world. Our true home is in heaven with God. While on this earth, our obligation is to do God's will. If the Lord's Prayer is to be meaningful to us, we cannot omit the words: "Thy will be done." Surely, we must be ready and willing when God calls us from this world. It is unseemly to think that any of us would be brought into the Lord's presence with sorrow and lamentation, not freely consenting to our departure from this earthly bondage, but constrained by necessity.

Conclusion

It is important that all of us be single-minded, firm in faith, steadfast in courage, ready to do God's will, whatever it may be. Banish the fear of death and think of the eternal life that follows it. That will show people that we really live our faith.

Mr. Louis Russel died on November 27, 1974, in Richmond, Virginia, at age 49. Until his death, he lived the longest of any person with a heart-transplant, nearly six years. What a courageous man he was! He taught school, and spent every spare moment visiting hospitals with heart patients, and lecturing them on hope. Shortly before he died, he said: "No one is entirely free who has not conquered the fear of death." _____ was a free person. He (She) had no fear of death or dying.

O gentle Jesus, grant him (her) eternal rest.

FORTIETH HOMILY

General

Extension of sympathy to the family

Introduction

The last words of our Divine Redeemer on the cross were not uttered in the weak voice of a dying man, but rather with the loud voice of a conquerer. Trusting Himself to His Father, Christ said: "Into your hands I commend my spirit." How many countless millions have pillowed their heads in those words when going to their final rest!

Application

My dear friends, I just can't imagine anything more consoling for and comforting to a family visited by grief over the death of a loved one than the thought that he (she) is at rest in the tender arms of his (her) loving Creator and Father. The firm foundation for such a feeling can be found in the Old Testament Book of Wisdom: "The souls of the just are in the hand of God: and the torment of death shall not touch them" (Wis. 3:1).

The words "the souls of the just" mean those who die justified, that is, those in the state of grace. It is a defined doctrine of the Church that the souls of the just, which, at the moment of death, are free from all guilt of sin, and of all temporal punishment due sin, directly enter heaven. Likewise, it is a defined doctrine that the souls of the just, which, in the moment of death, are burdened with venial sins, or temporal punishment due sins, are purified after death in purgatory. According to St. Robert Bellarmine, it is seldom that even pious persons escape purgatory. Here, then, is the importance of this funeral Mass, since it is being offered to God in suffrage for _____'s soul, it being, as Scripture says, "a holy and wholesome thought to pray for the dead that they may be loosed from their sins" (2 Macc. 12:46).

Let it be said that the souls in purgatory are precious in God's sight. They are saints "in waiting." They are members of one of the three branches of the Church. There is the Church Triumphant, comprised of those already in heaven. There is the Church Suffering, consisting of the souls in purgatory. Finally, there is the Church Militant, consisting of the baptized here on earth who are struggling to know, love, and serve God in this life and to merit eternal happiness in the next. This union of the three branches of the Church is termed the Communion of Saints.

We have already mentioned the consoling words from the Book of Wisdom to the effect that "the souls of the just are in the hand of God." Having explained what is meant by the words, "the souls of the just," let us consider the rest of the inspired text: "The souls of the just ARE IN THE HAND OF GOD."

What a thoroughly moving expression: "in the hand of God"! That concept brought great comfort to King David when the thought of his sins and failures swept over his soul, yet he cried out to God: "Into your hands I commend my spirit; you will redeem me, O Lord, O faithful God" (Ps. 31:6). We have already seen that the last words of our Lord before He died for us on the cross were: "Father, into your hands I commend my spirit" (Lk. 23:46). Those same words fell from the lips of countless saints like Stephen, Polycarp, and Bernard, and from the heart and lips of countless sinners down through the eons of time. Could there ever be a greater tribute of trust in our Eternal Father, an almighty and merciful Father whose hands give and gather!

What does one really hope for from helpful hands? Is it not strength, protection, and love? David could praise God for His strength, saying: "O Lord, God of hosts, who is like you? Mighty are you, O Lord" (Ps. 89:9). When David's enemies pressed in on him, he cried to God in hope: "But you, O Lord, are my shield; my glory, you lift up my head! I fear not the myriads of people arrayed against me on every side. Rise up, O Lord! Save me, my God!" (Ps. 3:4, 7, 8) Who can doubt the depths of God's love for us, the God who sent His own Divine Son to become Man and die on the cross to ransom us from our sins, and open heaven to the just?

Conclusion

_____ is in the powerful, protective, and loving hands of a tender Father. His (Her) immortal soul, we piously hope, is enjoying the Beatific Vision. The mortal remains we bless today can never again be touched by death. What a comfort for us to read in God's Word: "The souls of the just are in the hand of God: and the torment of death shall not touch them." May each of us so live our days on earth as to be worthy of seeing God in heaven, worshiping, thanking, and loving Him for all eternity.

_____, remember us and our needs at the throne of God. Amen.

FORTY-FIRST HOMILY

General

Extension of sympathy to the family

Introduction

St. Frederick was chosen Bishop of Utrecht in 825. In the discharge of his pastoral duties he found it necessary to reprimand the Empress, wife of Louis the Debonair, incurring thereby her resentment and fury. On July 18, 838, after the saint had celebrated Holy Mass, and while making his thanksgiving, he was stabbed by two hired assassins. The saintly bishop died within fifteen minutes, reciting over and over verse 9 from Psalm 116: "I shall walk before the Lord in the land of the living." Death, you see, to St. Frederick was not the end of living, but rather the beginning of a new and eternal life with God.

Application

It must seem extremely strange to the family, relatives, and friends of _____, gathered around his (her) casket at his (her) funeral Mass, to hear the celebrant say: "_____ is not dead, but he (she) walks before the Lord in the land of the living." Strange or not, it is the truth. Every time we recite the Profession of Faith at Sunday Mass, we say: "We look for the resurrection of the dead, and life in the world to come." Now, we must put our faith into practice.

Not for one instant since _____'s soul disentangled itself from his (her) body at God's command, has that soul ceased to be alive. The Old Testament Book of Wisdom says explicitly: "The souls of the just are in the hand of God: no torment shall touch them. They seemed in the view of the foolish, to be dead; and their passing away was thought an affliction and their going forth from us, utter destruction. But they are in peace" (Wis. 3:1–3).

Before the creation of angels and human beings, God was perfectly happy. He needed nothing to add to His happiness. It was out of goodness that God created the spiritual beings we call angels, and human beings, who are composed of material bodies and spiritual souls. Since God is a Spirit, He created for each of us a spiritual soul which is an image of Himself. The reason God created angels and mankind is best set forth by St. Irenaeus, who wrote that God did not need angels or man to add to His happiness; rather, He felt the need of beings upon whom to bestow His gifts. Oh, the goodness of God! "With age-old love have I loved you, so I kept my mercy toward you" (Jer. 31:3). To have God as our heavenly Father, to give Him all the glory possible, to keep His commandments, to love Him above all things on this earth, and to be happy with Him forever in heaven—this constitutes the end and purpose of our creation.

When our first parents disobeyed a solemn prohibition by their Creator, the punishment was swift. They lost sanctifying grace; heaven was closed to them and their descendants; and they were expelled from the Garden of Eden. The loss of God's friendship was a towering blow. As a result of the sin of Adam and Eve, man's intellect was darkened and his will weakened; and death became the lot of saints and sinners. In spite of Adam and Eve's failure to obey God's commandement, God did not abandon them. He gave them the seed of hope that a ransomer would be sent to help them. In the years that became centuries, the patriarchs and prophets kept the promise of a future Messiah before the Chosen People. At last, when He came, who was the Savior but God's own Divine Son, Jesus Christ born Man from the Blessed Virgin Mary? "Yes, God so loved the world that he gave his only Son, that whoever believes in him may not die but may have eternal life" (Jn. 3:16).

The coming of God's Divine Son made Man, His living with us on this earth for thirty-three years, and His cruel death on the cross to redeem us, is a love story beyond all telling. What would have happened to mankind had Christ *not* come? The answer is too terrible to contemplate. St. Augustine tells us that, had our Lord not been born in time, we would all have suffered eternal death. All of us would have suffered everlasting unhappiness, had it not been for His mercy. Not one human being would have been raised to life from the grave, had Christ not shared our death. All of us would have perished, had He not come.

Conclusion

Our Lord Jesus, Son of God made Man, is present in the tabernacle; and in a few moments the same Christ will be a Victim offering Himself to His Father as He did on Calvary, pleading mercy and forgiveness for the soul of _____. Let us pour out our thanksgiving to our Lord for bringing him (her) salvation and redemption. As St. Frederick did, we can hope that he (she) is walking "before the Lord, in the land of the living" (Ps. 16:9).

Eternal rest grant unto him (her), O Lord, and let perpetual light shine upon him (her). May he (she) rest in peace. Amen.

FORTY-SECOND HOMILY

General

Extension of sympathy to the family

Introduction

Blessed William Cufitellia was a Franciscan Tertiary who became a hermit near Scicli in Sicily, and spent seventy years in a tiny cell, giving himself up to prayer and penance. His food consisted, for the most part, of vegetables he grew in a small garden. Many thousands through the years sought his guidance and spiritual direction. In 1411, when Blessed William was ninety-five years of age, the church bells in the area began to ring by themselves one day; and the people of Scicli went to find out what caused the brilliant light surrounding the hermitage of the pious monk. Arriving, they found the old hermit dead on his knees, hands joined in prayer, and his mortal remains bathed in beams of light.

Application

The miraculous ringing of bells and the phenomenon of light announcing the deaths of saintly men and women appear in the lives of the saints from time to time. Holy Scripture tells us of extraordinary light in relation to God's power and glory. For instance, when Moses was on Mt. Sinai to receive God's law for the Chosen People, the whole top of the mountain seemed to be on fire; and while Moses did not see God face to face, speaking to him only through a cloud, nevertheless, the glory of God was reflected in the patriarch's face. When Moses came down from the mountain, his face shone like the sun; and the people had to ask him to veil his face.

When our Blessed Lord was transfigured on Mt. Tabor before Sts. Peter, James, and John, St. Matthew records that Christ "was transfigured before their eyes. His face became as dazzling as the sun, his clothes as radiant as light" (Matt. 17:2). St. Luke, when recording the Transfiguration, describes Moses and Elias, who spoke with the Messiah, as men "appearing in glory" (Lk. 9:31). When "a cloud" overshadowed the three disciples, they "grew fearful as the others entered it" (Lk. 9:34). St. Paul's conversion was initiated by "a light from the sky [that] suddenly flashed around him" (Acts 9:3); and the experience of speaking with the hidden Christ on that road to Damascus left the future Apostle a shaken and trembling man with a blindness that lasted for three days.

One has no difficulty in accepting the Word of God relative to the power and glory of God. St. Paul tells us "that God dwells in unapproachable *light*, whom no human being has ever seen or can see" (1 Tim. 6:16). The same St. Paul could say of heaven: "Eye has not seen, ear has not heard, nor has it so much as dawned on man what God has prepared for those who love him" (1 Cor. 2:9).

Theologians state plainly that heaven is an abode of everlasting joy. The most awesome joy is that of seeing God in all His glory. The vision of God is the source of everlasting happiness. The supernatural beatitude of heaven fundamentally consists in the intuitive vision of the Divine Essence. As the Divine Essence subsists in three distinct Persons, the Beatific Vision involves the intuitive knowledge of the Blessed Trinity. Needless to say, the human intellect cannot attain to this exalted knowledge by its own power, but requires for this purpose a special "light of glory," which is a divine operation. As a consequence of the "light of glory," the soul entering heaven sees God as He is (1 Jn. 3:2) and "face to face" (1 Cor. 13:12). The blessed in heaven can neither suffer pain nor commit sin. St. Augustine could say that it is easier to name the evils from which the blessed are free than to count up their joys.

Conclusion

Reflect carefully on what you have heard this morning and tell me if this is a day for tears or a day for rejoicing? The soul of _____ _____ has been called home to be with God for all eternity in heaven. These mortal remains will rise from the grave at the end of the world, to be reunited with the soul; and both together will be with God for ever and ever.

We began by stating that when Blessed William Cufitellia died, a bright light shone around his saintly body. Holy Scripture tells us that the just in heaven have a radiance and beauty called "clarity." Our Lord assures us: "Then the saints will shine like the sun in their Father's kingdom!" (Matt. 13:43)

It is the fervent hope of each of us that the soul of _____ _____ is already in God's presence; however, should the justice of God require a delay for a time, then let us hasten his (her) union with God by our Masses, said or heard, our Holy Communions, prayers, and alms. This would be the real test of our abiding love.

May he (she) rest in the hands of God. May eternal light shine upon him (her). Amen.

FORTY-THIRD HOMILY

General

Extension of sympathy to the family

Introduction

It is said that, when the illustrious St. Charles Cardinal Borromeo was dying, he requested that three pictures be hung in his sickroom where he could see them from his bed. The first picture he asked for was that of the agony of our Lord in the Garden of Gethsemane. The second was a picture of the burial of Christ in the borrowed tomb, familiar to all of us as the Fourteenth Station of the Way of the Cross. The third picture the ailing Cardinal asked for was that of the Resurrection of our Sacred Redeemer from the dead on the first Easter Sunday.

Application

My dear friends, I have no way of knowing what those three pictures meant to St. Charles, individually or collectively; but they surely must have inspired thoughts of Christ's love and mercy for sinners; for by dying and being buried, Christ shared mankind's greatest burden and became victorious over death; finally, in Christ's resurrection from the dead is the promise of our resurrection from the grave on the last day.

Gathered here as we are today for the funeral Mass for the repose of the soul of _____, let us pray that he (she) is with God in eternal bliss. Let us ask him (her) to intercede for us that we may garner instruction and comfort from our consideration of the agony of our Lord in the Garden of Gethsemane, His burial, and His glorious resurrection from the dead. Every funeral we attend must be for us a stark reminder of our own mortality. We too, like _____ _____, must submit to the universal law of death imposed upon all mankind as the result of the sin of our first parents. The time, the nature and the place of our death are known only to God. The observations made in this homily are designed to bring solace to the bereaved members of the family of the deceased, and to each of us a deeper faith, a stronger hope, and a consuming love for our holy Redeemer, who became Man so that we could become children of God and heirs to the kingdom of heaven. Let us open our hearts to the following lessons.

I. *THE AGONY OF CHRIST IN THE GARDEN OF GETHSEMANE*

Consider that when the Last Supper had taken place, at which our Lord had instituted the Holy Eucharist and spoken glowingly of His commandment to the disciples to love one another, and of His approaching death, Christ led the Apostles to the Garden of Gethsemane to pray, as was His wont. Eight of the Apostles were told to wait for Him at a distance. Peter, James, and John, who had witnessed His glorious Transfiguration on Mount Tabor, He brought a bit closer to Him; and they heard Him say: "My heart is nearly broken with sorrow. Remain here and stay awake with me" (Matt. 26:38). Christ went on a stone's throw by Himself and fell prostrate in prayer.

What brought on the paroxysm of sorrow, anguish, and fear that pressed Him face down on the ground? As God, He knew in detail every indignity, every mental and physical suffering He would have to endure in His passion and painful crucifixion. Too, every horrible sin ever committed in the past, present, and future, the sins of all mankind, your sins and mine, were heaped upon the sinless Christ there in the garden. Finally, there was the knowledge that, in spite of all He would suffer, souls would continue to be lost for all eternity. Judas, one of His own Apostles, at that very moment was completing a deal to betray Him to His enemies for thirty pieces of silver. Small wonder that Christ's sweat became drops of blood, or that in His agony He cried out: "My Father, if it is possible, let this cup pass me by. Still, let it be as you would have it, not as I" (Matt. 26:39).

The agony of Christ in the garden points up two great lessons: first, the depth of Christ's love for man that He would die so cruel a death to ransom him from an unhappy eternity, and open heaven so he could be with God. The second lesson is Christ's reverence for and compliance with the will of His Eternal Father. Let us always accept God's will in all things, saying: "Thy will be done on earth."

II. *BURIAL OF CHRIST*

In our day, the importance of a person is often judged by the number of people who attend his or her funeral. When Christ was buried, although He was the Son of God and went about this earth doing good, raising the dead to life, curing the sick, giving sight to the blind, and whose death on the cross saved mankind, reopened heaven, paid the debt of our sins and conquered death—despite all this, maybe no more than twelve persons, including His afflicted Mother, took part in Christ's burial in the borrowed tomb. Oh, the shame of it all! In being buried, Christ identified Himself with what will take place after this Mass, the sad interment.

III. *CHRIST'S RESURRECTION FROM THE DEAD*

Christ foretold that He would rise from the dead three days after His death on Calvary. He did rise on Easter Sunday in proof of His divinity. His rising, His promise gave full assurance all of us will rise from the grave on the last day! This truth comforted St. Charles Borromeo, and it should comfort those in sorrow today.

Conclusion

Lord, by Your cross and resurrection You have set us free. You are the Savior of the world!

FORTY-FOURTH HOMILY

For an exemplary Catholic

Extension of sympathy to the family

Introduction

Charles Carroll of Carrollton, Md., one of the original signers of the Declaration of Independence, was all his life a practical Catholic. He lived for many years after the new republic became a reality, and on his deathbed he took the time to enumerate his many blessings. Having lived into his ninety-sixth year, he was grateful for having been blessed with good health, wealth, property, and all the other good things of life. He was not unmindful of the public approbation and esteem accorded him during his long life. Having run through a veritable litany of blessings, he paused for a moment, as if to give greater emphasis to what he was about to say. He told those standing around his bed that the thing that gave him the greatest satisfaction and consolation was that he had always practiced the duties of his holy religion as well as he could, which to him was a joy and never a burden.

Application

Gathered as we are today for the funeral of _____, the grief resulting from his (her) passing from this life is shared by all of us. To his (her) immediate family, one of the consoling things that must temper the loss is the knowledge that he (she) was a practical and practicing Catholic *par excellence*. His (Her) religion was never like a coat to be put on or taken off to suit the occasion; indeed, it was an unchangeable and permanent quality of his (her) life. What he (she) determined to be the teaching of the Church, he (she) embraced; and it became a matter of conscience for him (her). His (Her) devotion to the Mass, his (her) frequentation of the sacraments was edifying, setting an example for the family and the Catholic community as well. Surely, there is comfort for the family in the words of our Lord Himself: "Whoever acknowledges me before men, I will acknowledge before my Father in heaven" (Matt. 10:32).

What may puzzle some is why a thoroughly good person like _____ had to suffer before his (her) death. In God's providence, the illness and distress which often precede death can be said to be a complete atonement for all our sins, provided our death is united to the death of Christ. Such a death has the power of satisfaction for sin. A truly Christian death is the normal and the efficacious mode of paying to God what is technically termed "the debt of temporal punishment," evidenced by the very words in which God announced to our first parents the results of their sin. Above all, we must consider the death of the Christian who willingly and consciously accepts the chastisement in union with Christ's death, to be, after the sacraments, the most potent cleansing of man's soul. Thus, there is in death the possibility of justice and satisfaction which goes beyond its penal character.

The fact that Christ, the very Son of God, died and was buried, has to play a large part in the death of a Christian. If God's own Divine Son suffered a cruel death on the cross, if He was at one time among the dead, death cannot any longer be an unmitigated evil; to die and be buried cannot be a hopeless and desperate condition; to die cannot be any more a nightmare of terror. In the Epistle to the Hebrews, we come upon these inspired words:

> Now, since the children are men of blood and flesh, Jesus likewise had a full share in ours, that by his death he might rob the devil, the prince of death, of his power, and free those who through fear of death had been slaves their whole life long . . . therefore, he had to become like his brothers in every way, that he might be a merciful and faithful high priest before God on their behalf, to expiate the sins of the people. Since he was himself tested through what he suffered, he is able to help those who are tested (Heb. 2:14–18).

There is no question but that in the death of Christ there was that supreme value of satisfaction to the justice of God through which we have confidence in God both in life and in death. There is, as well, the aspect of example to a high degree in Christ's bridging the deep gap between life and death. "While we live," says St. Paul, "we are responsible to the Lord, and when we die we die as his servants. Both in life and in death we are the Lord's" (Rom. 14:8–9).

Conclusion

I am confident that Charles Carroll besought the prayers of his family and friends for the grace of a holy and peaceful death, as did _____ _____ before he (she) died. Let us continue praying for him (her) in the Mass, and in our evening prayers. It is very moving to read what St. Ephrem said to those around him shortly before he died: "I conjure you in God's Holy Name to remember me: let your prayers aid me, and wipe away the dust scattered in my eyes, and I will rise and give thanks to Him who raises us from the dead."

Lord, by Your cross and resurrection You have set us free. You are the Savior of the world. Amen.

FORTY-FIFTH HOMILY

General

Extension of sympathy to the family

Introduction

St. Stephen was abbot of a monastery near Rieta in Italy, and a man of remarkable piety. Pope St. Gregory the Great mentioned him several times in his writings, especially about the abbot's death. The saintly Pope Gregory related that eye-witnesses had testified that they saw angels standing around his bed when he was dying, and that after he died, they saw angels carrying his immortal soul heavenwards, surrounded by a brilliant light.

Application

My dear friends, ever since _____ was baptized, he (she) had his (her) own special guardian angel. According to the general teaching of the theologians, not only every baptized person, but every human being, including unbelievers, has his or her special guardian angel from birth. St. Jerome comments on the teaching of our Lord that His disciples should not despise the children who came to him, since, as He said: "For I say to you that their angels in heaven always see the face of my Father" (Matt. 18:10). St. Jerome said: "How great is the value of the human soul that every single person from birth received an angel for his (her) protection."

This being so, one may wonder why any person ever sins. In answer to that, one must remember that man has free will, and, as St. Thomas says about the effectiveness of angelic tutelage, man is free to act against good inspirations of a guardian angel, just as man can act against his conscience.

It is said that the primary task of the angels is the glorification and the service of God. In relation to man, the secondary task of angels is the protection of mankind and the care for their salvation. Guardian angels are like shepherds guarding their flocks. They put good thoughts in our mind and move our will to do what is right, without, however, destroying our free will. They offer our prayers and good works to God. St. Thomas taught that guardian angels offer their prayers with man's, and thus make them more pleasing to God. Oh, how much God must love us, to give each of us a powerful spirit to guard us in this life!

Imagine the protective energy exercised by the guardian angel for a person who is nearing the end of his or her earthly pilgrimage. Saintly writers tell us that the forces of evil, Satan and the fallen angels, do all they can to induce the dying to doubt the infinite mercy of God, and thus move them to despair of God's merciful forgiveness for the numerous sins committed in a whole lifetime. It must have been a great source of comfort for St. Stephen, the abbot, to have seen angels surrounding his deathbed, knowing they were there to ward off the evil influences of Satan and the fallen angels, denying them a final victory. We believe that our guardian angel, although unseen, is near us, helping us to ward off the bad influence of evil spirits.

One can only imagine the joy of "mission accomplished" experienced by a guardian angel who escorts the soul of a justified human being into the presence of God in heaven. St. Paul asked the rhetorical question about angels with the built-in answer: "Are they not all ministering spirits, sent to serve those who are to inherit salvation?" (Heb. 1:14)

Conclusion

It is our confident hope that _____'s guardian angel has joyfully escorted his (her) noble soul into the glorious presence of Almighty God in heaven. Even at this funeral Mass, other angels are present for this Holy Sacrifice, as they are at every Mass. In the First Eucharistic Prayer, the celebrant calls upon angelic service in this prayer:

> Almighty God, we pray that your angel may take this sacrifice to your altar in heaven. Then, as we receive from this altar the sacred Body and Blood of your Son, let us be filled with every grace and blessing through Christ our Lord. Amen.

In a little while, as the mortal remains are being lowered into the earth to await the resurrection on the last day, the angels are again invoked in the Song of Farewell in these words: "May Christ, who called you, take you to Himself; may angels lead you to Abraham's side." Some ritual prayers petition God to send angels to guard the graves of our dear departed until the last day. What greater tribute could be paid to the worth of one justified child of God!

In the Book of Tobit, we learn that God sent an angel disguised in human form in answer to Tobit's prayers for help. The angel helped Tobit's son Tobias to reclaim the family fortune, helped restore Tobit's eyesight, and found a saintly wife for Tobias. Father and son wanted to pay him for his services, but the angel said:

> Thank God! Give him the praise and the glory. Before all the living, acknowledge the many good things he has done for you, by blessing and extolling his name in song. Before all men, honor and proclaim God's deeds, and do not slack in praising him (Tobit. 12:6).

After saying that, the angel revealed that he was Raphael, one of seven angels who enter and serve before the glory of the Lord.

Let all of us thank God today for His goodness in sending His angels to help _____ save his (her) soul. May the angels lead him (her) to paradise. Amen.

FORTY-SIXTH HOMILY

For parents who have lost a son or daughter

Extension of sympathy to the family

Introduction

Abraham was one of the great patriarchs of the Old Testament. St. Paul in his Letter to the Hebrews strikes the keynote of the life of Abraham, saying that he was destined to be a sojourner, a stranger, and pilgrim on this earth en route to a celestial home with God in heaven (Heb. 11:13).

Application

From the time of Abraham's call to serve his God, hard things were required of him. His will was to be sacrificed to the will of God. While he was in Haran, God said to him: "Go forth from the land of your kinsfolk and from your father's house to a land I will show you" (Gen. 12:1). That in itself was a great personal sacrifice when we remember how sacred and strong were the familial ties of the Hebrews. That hardship was but an additional distress to Abraham, since he was childless. In spite of everything, Abraham went forth, never again to return home, going among aliens and enemies, a stranger in strange lands. The one thing that supported him was God's promise of help: "Fear not, Abram! I am your shield; I will make your reward very great" (Gen. 15:1).

God kept His promise to Abraham, blessing him with material riches, but withholding the fulfillment of the promise of children to him and to his wife Sarah. After a century of wayfaring, it took greater effort to sustain the hope that God's promise would be fulfilled. In God's good time, a son was born to Abraham and Sarah, and he was named Isaac.

God loved Abraham dearly, and He wanted to test Abraham's love for Him. The patriarch had stood up well under the long exile, toil, poverty, riches, seductions by heathenism, and the like, but how would he react to a test that would involve the life of his long-awaited son Isaac, who was then approaching manhood? But God's order was clear: "Take your son Isaac, your only one, whom you love, and go to the land of Moriah. There you shall offer him up as a holocaust on a height that I will point out to you" (Gen. 22:2).

Early the next morning, Abraham and his son Isaac and two servants set out on a two-day journey to the place God told him to go. A donkey was loaded with the wood Abraham had himself cut for the sacrifice. The servants were ordered to wait where they were; then Abraham placed the wood on Isaac's shoulders, while he carried the torch and the sacrificial knife as they climbed to the spot indicated by God. Isaac asked his father where the lamb was for the sacrifice, but Abraham said God would provide one. Reaching the place where the sacrifice was to take place, Abraham built an altar and set the wood in place, lit it and next tied up Isaac and placed him on the altar. As the broken-hearted father raised the knife over his head, the Lord's messenger called to him, "Abraham, Abraham! Do not lay a hand on the boy . . . I know now how devoted you are to God, since you did not withhold from me your beloved son . . . God will bless you abundantly" (Gen. 22:1–17).

Abraham had been tested, and his love for God more than amply proven. As he saw a ram entangled in a thicket and recognized in it a substitute victim for the holocaust, the sacrifice that followed must have been a joyous one of thanksgiving on the part of Abraham.

Conclusion

My dear friends, I have placed before you a man, a chosen patriarch, whose mind had grasped the truth that we are all pilgrims and wanderers in this life, making our way to another and better life with God in heaven; or as St. Paul puts it: "Indeed, we know that when this earthly tent in which we dwell is destroyed, we have a dwelling provided for us by God, a dwelling in the heavens not made by hands, but to last forever" (2 Cor. 5:1).

Sharp as were the other tests of Abraham's faith during his long life, the most crucial and painful test was the one involving his willingness to sacrifice his own beloved son in obedience to the divine will of God. Dear parents of _____, I am sure your holy faith has undergone rugged tests during your combined lives, but none, thus far, can compare to the test of faith imposed on you these last days by the will of God in calling your son (daughter) from this life. Obedient acceptance of God's holy will in this heartbreaking trial is the greatest test of your faith. Without strength from God, do you think Abraham could have ever raised his hand with that sacrificial knife in it with total submission to God's will? Believe me, that same strength is available to you today.

During this funeral Mass for _____, make that act of resignation and submission to God's will, and somehow you will hear God say: "I know now how devoted you are to God since you did not withold from me your own beloved son (daughter). I will make your reward very great." Amen.

FORTY-SEVENTH HOMILY

General

Extension of sympathy to the family

Introduction

It has to be an unthinking person who would dare to remark that there are not too many texts in Holy Scripture that would bring consolation to those in bereavement over the loss of a loved one. Anyone who could make such a statement bespeaks unfamiliarity with the Word of God. What about the Old Testament Book of Wisdom, the Gospels, and the letters of St. Paul—First and Second Corinthians, Timothy, and Hebrews? Personally, were there not another text besides this one from the Book of Revelation, it would suffice: "Happy now are the dead who die in the Lord!" The Spirit added, "Yes, they shall find rest from their labors, for their good works accompany them" (Rev. 14:13). Let us consider this text prayerfully.

Application

I. "HAPPY NOW ARE THE DEAD WHO DIE IN THE LORD"

The first requisite for anyone to die in the Lord is to have been baptized. It is our Lord Himself who tells us that we must receive spiritual regeneration through baptism, and that, without it, we cannot enter the kingdom of heaven. Here are Christ's words to Nicodemus: "I solemnly assure you, no one can enter into God's kingdom without being begotten of water and Spirit" (Jn. 3:5). By baptism, the soul is adjusted toward God in a supernaturally perfect and complete relation of innocence and favor, for not only is original sin washed away, but all actual sins as well, and all temporal punishments due to them. By being born again through water and the Holy Spirit, we are assured of the reception of the gift of sanctifying grace, the infused theological virtues of faith, hope, and charity, and the gifts of the Holy Spirit. Through baptism, we are made the adopted children of God and heirs of the kingdom of heaven, be it by baptism of water, of desire, or of blood.

We really should be embarrassed by thinking of God's endless benefactions to us during our lifetime, the sacraments placed at our disposal, especially the sacraments of the Holy Eucharist and penance; the Holy Sacrifice of the Mass; the guide posts of the ten commandments; and the teachings of the Church down through the years of our life. God, in His infinite mercy, encompasses the whole life of the Christian, which begins with baptism and is complemented by the sacrament of the last anointing which, worthily received at the hour of death, prepares us for immediate entrance into everlasting happiness with God. Happy are the saints and repentant sinners who die in the Lord!

II. *"YES, THEY SHALL FIND REST FROM THEIR LABORS"*

Note how the Holy Spirit proclaims that the dead who die in the Lord rest from their labors; they are happy in their rest; they rest from all sin, temptation, sorrow, pain, or suffering. Never again can sorrow touch them. The Christians who die in the Lord shall have, as the Psalmist says, "their fill of the prime gifts of your house; from your delightful stream you give them to drink" (Ps. 36:9).

"The present life," says St. Gregory the Great, "in comparison to everlasting bliss, is more like death than life." It is the vision of God that is the source of untold happiness. Let us not grieve for _____ _____; rather, let us thank God for having taken him (her) to Himself to enjoy eternal bliss in heaven. Take comfort from these words of our Lord, the promise He made to all of us: "Come to me, all you who are weary and find life burdensome, and I will refresh you . . . Your souls will find rest" (Matt. 11:28).

III. *THE WORKS OF THOSE WHO DIE IN THE LORD "WILL FOLLOW THEM"*

It is a doctrine of the Church that the just in heaven see the Triune God, yet some see Him more perfectly than others (Council of Florence). The knowledge and love of God may be greater in one saint than in another, and the same is true of the joys of heaven. The degree of glory in heaven depends on the amount of sanctifying grace a person has at the moment of death. When death comes, the time for meriting is over. As Scripture says: "Whether a tree falls to the south or to the north, wherever it falls, there shall it lie" (Eccles. 11:3). All in heaven are happy, but some will have more glory than others. St. Paul tells us, "The sun has a splendor of its own, so has the moon, and the stars have theirs. Even among the stars one differs from another in brightness. So it is with the resurrection of the dead" (1 Cor. 15:41–42). There is no envy in heaven, since the blessed are all children of one Father and have their portion from Him (Matt. 20).

Conclusion

Dear members of the family of _____, how consoling it must be to recall how diligent he (she) was in fulfilling his (her) religious obligations, his (her) exemplary life, his (her) support for works of the parish (and the school). How full his (her) hands will be with good works when he (she) stands before our Blessed Lord to hear Him say: "Come. You have my Father's blessing! Inherit the kingdom prepared for you from the creation of the world" (Matt. 25:31).

Truly, we can say of the deceased: "Happy the dead who die in the Lord." He (She) has gone to his (her) reward.

FORTY-EIGHTH HOMILY

Death with tragic circumstances

Extension of sympathy to the family

Introduction

St. Peter of Verona received the religious habit from the hands of St. Dominic himself. He was a man of great promise. In spite of his brilliance as a scholar and preacher, he was a humble man who loved to care for the sick and always volunteered to perform the most menial work in the priory. God put his humility to a very great test. He suffered for a long time under the cruel cross of false accusation until his innocence was vindicated in God's own time.

In a post to which St. Peter was appointed by Pope Gregory IX, he did his work well; and in the doing, he suffered bitter emnity. While preaching on Palm Sunday, 1252, he told the crowd that his life was in jeopardy, and that a price had been put on his head. "Let them do their worst," he added; "I shall be more powerful dead than alive." Two weeks later, on April 6, 1252, the saint was waylaid by an assassin and mortally wounded by blows to his head. He remained conscious for some time. He joyfully commended his soul to God and prayed for his murderer, as Christ did on the cross, and as St. Stephen did for those who stoned him to death. When he could no longer speak, he traced on the ground, with a finger dipped in his own blood, the words: *"Credo in Deum"*—"I believe in God." St. Peter proved his power after death, for his murderer, one year later, filled with remorse and repentance, abjured his heresy, became a Dominican lay-brother, and died so holy a death that his memory was venerated.

Application

My dear friends, this thumbnail sketch of the life of Saint Peter of Verona contains lessons well designed to bring comfort to the family of the late _____ in their grief. First, we must all be convinced of God's love for each of us, and His desire for our eternal salvation. Everything that happens to us proceeds from the infinite wisdom and power of God, and is directed for our salvation. At times, it is difficult to see God's hand in suffering imposed upon us by the malice of others, such as in the false accusations made against St. Peter. We might be tempted to question God's hand in the pain and suffering of a loved one, forgetting that Christ's pain, suffering, and death were the means He used to redeem the world and to open heaven to all who seek entrance. It is in the face of great trials that we must force ourselves to see that God's will is mercy itself, and that things that happen to us are either willed or permitted by God Himself, as part of the plan for our salvation. Firm assent to this will be for the members of the family of _____ the best safeguard against grudging acceptance or rebellion.

The second point I submit for your prayerful consideration is also taken from the life of St. Peter of Verona. It was his unalterable conviction that the time or the manner of his death was of no personal concern to him, since, as he said, "I shall be more powerful dead than alive." To those who feel poignantly the loss of the love, counsel, companionship, and guidance of _____, I hasten to assure them that such things are not lost to them. With St. Peter, the deceased can say in all truth: "I shall be more powerful dead than alive." We are as close to our justified dead as the shortest prayer we utter. St. Paul says: "Love never fails" (I Cor. 13:8). Our deceased relatives and friends who are in heaven are always pleading for us at the throne of God (Rev. 8:4), and often save us from danger. St. Catherine of Bologna (1463) used to call upon the Holy Souls when the saints seemed to be tardy in helping her, and she never asked them in vain.

Finally, who could fail to be impressed by the deep and abiding faith of St. Peter of Verona, who, when unable any longer to speak, traced his profession of faith in his own blood in the dust of the road: "*Credo in Deum.* I believe in God"? How consoled the family of _____ _____ should be, knowing that he (she) died fortified with the sacraments. His (Her) whole life was a veritable profession of faith. "Whoever acknowledges me before men, I will acknowledge before my Father in heaven" (Matt. 10:32). He (She) has gone to his (her) eternal reward.

Conclusion

When the publisher of a noted European literary magazine died, a memorial tribute began with this observation: "The mystery of living is defined by dying." We were made by God to know, love, and serve Him in this life and to be happy with Him in the next life. Death frees the soul from the body at the end of our pilgrimage here on earth, and the soul goes to its judgment, while the body returns to the earth to await the resurrection on the last day.

In the presence of death here today, let each of us resolve to pray daily for the grace of a happy death. With a heart full of love for God, and a soul full of sanctifying grace, death will have no terror for us. _____, may you "rest in peace!" Amen.

FORTY-NINTH HOMILY

General

Extension of sympathy to the family

Introduction

Archbishop Audu was the venerable patriarch of the Chaldeans during the First Vatican Council. He never tired of telling how he was converted to the faith. It seems that in his youth he was bent on enjoying every worldly pleasure he could discover. One day, on one of his excursions, he happened to visit a Chaldean monastery. As he was entering the grounds under a massive arched gateway, the keystone of the arch fell and severely wounded him. During his long convalescence in the monastery, he devoted much of his time to reading pious books. So profoundly was he affected by the instruction and the example of the monks that he left the sacred retreat as a well-instructed and fervent Christian. Afterwards he studied for the priesthood, was ordained, later was named archbishop and, eventually, became the patriarch of the Chaldean Catholics.

Application

My dear friends, we are gathered here today to offer the Holy Sacrifice of the Mass for the blissful repose of the soul of _____ _____, a soul we have every right to hope is already in God's presence in heaven. If, in God's infinite justice, this union is delayed, we can hope that this august Sacrifice of the Mass will open the gates of heaven for him (her).

Perhaps, for the family and relatives the one word "*Why*" takes on immense proportions today: "Why was _____ taken?" "Why was he (she) taken when he (she) was so sorely needed by the family?" I ask the Holy Spirit, the Comforter, to make me His instrument so that I can, through the balm of faith, heal your wounded hearts and move you to say, as our Blessed Lord said in His awful agony: "Father, if it is your will, take this cup from me: yet not my will but yours be done" (Lk. 22:42). On our Lord's part, the will of His Father was paramount. On our part, God's will must always be paramount. Let me present to you now a few reasons why we must always accept God's will with resignation.

First, nothing happens to us without either the will or the permission of God. If, as the Scriptures tell us, "Not a single sparrow falls to the ground without your Father's consent" (Matt. 10:29), then, surely, nothing can happen to us without His consent.

The great Old Testament character Joseph, whose history is recorded in the Book of Genesis, saw clearly the hand of God in what he had to endure. His brothers envied him because of his father's love for him, so they planned to kill him, but decided rather to sell their brother as a slave to merchants going to Egypt. Years later, when a great famine struck the land of Israel, the brothers went to Egypt to buy corn. Imagine the amazement and the alarm of the brothers when they confronted their exiled brother Joseph in the house of the Pharaoh. Far from showing resentment, Joseph embraced his wicked brothers, saying to them: "So it was not really you, but God who had me come here; and he has made me a father to Pharaoh, lord of all his household, and ruler over the whole of the land of Egypt" (Gen. 45:8). Joseph saw the providential hand of God in the agony he had endured as a slave.

Secondly, we must be convinced that the crosses and trials we have to endure in this life are not sent through hatred or caprice, but out of love for us. Who could ever be as dear to God the Father as His only-begotten Son, who was one in being with the Father, and the splendor of His glory? This Christ is He of whom the Eternal Father said: "This is my beloved Son. My favor rests on him" (Matt. 3:17). Nevertheless, this very Son of God, "the Man of sorrows," would die a cruel death on the cross and be buried in a borrowed grave. Could anyone here this morning call pain, suffering, or even death, evil, since Christ Himself endured them to ransom mankind and open heaven to all those who die in His favor? Death we all face, and no one can escape it; and it is comforting to know that Christ did not exempt Himself or His own Blessed Mother. There were sad circumstances in our Lord's death that few remember. He was only thirty-three years old when He died on the cross, and He had to leave behind Him His beloved widowed Mother who would survive Him and be dependent on others for her protection and support.

Conclusion

Since the fall of our first parents, every human being must submit to death at the time and place willed by God. Scripture says that only the foolish think of death as an affliction or utter destruction. The Word of God states plainly that the dead who are found worthy of heaven are in peace (Wis. 3:1–6).

Let us all acknowledge God's holy will as mercy itself, and resign ourselves to it in all things, saying as Christ taught us in the Our Father: "Thy will be done on earth as it is in heaven."

FIFTIETH HOMILY

General

Extension of sympathy to the family

Introduction

It is said that those who have made specialized studies of the epitaphs found in the catacombs agree that two expressions are frequently used to indicate the cherished beliefs of the early Christians relative to their dead.

The first, "in peace," is repeated on many tombs. The words convey the lesson that those who die in the Lord are at rest from conflict, fear, and apprehension: "But they are in peace" (Wis. 3:3).

The second expression frequently gracing the tombs is: "alive with God." The Word of God declares: "And the souls of the just are in the hand of God" (Wis. 3:1).

Application

After two thousand years we have no deeper hope! Sad to say, so many of us become so attached to our life here on earth that we are prone to forget that we have been placed on this earth to know, love, and serve God in this life and to be happy with Him in heaven for all eternity. We are pilgrims on this earth. Heaven is our true home.

Man is a wondrous combination of a material body and a spiritual and immortal soul. Man's body is animated by a principle whose essence and activity are not circumscribed by the limits of matter. With other animals, man shares the faculties of instinct and sense; but what elevates him above lower animals is his spiritual and immortal soul. Man's intelligence, free will, and memory permit him, alone above all the lower animals, to form a concept of moral good and to know God, albeit in an imperfect manner, in this life. Scripture says: "You have made him [man] little less than the angels, and crowned him with glory and honor" (Ps. 8:6).

God is the end of all creation; and since He made all things for His glory, the more perfect they are, the more they redound to the glory of the Creator. Man was made to know, love, and serve God in this life, and to be happy with Him in the next: "O Lord our God, you are worthy to receive glory and honor and power! For you have created all things; by your will they came to be and were made" (Rev. 4:11). Man's spiritual and immortal soul is the principle of life for his material body. Through the sin of our first parents, every child is born into this world with the stain of that original sin on his or her soul, save our Lord and His holy Mother. Through baptism, the soul is flooded with sanctifying grace which removes original sin, and any other sins; and the soul becomes pleasing to God. Through baptism we are made children of God and heirs of the kingdom of heaven.

St. Louis of France used to say that he thought more of the tiny chapel in which he had been baptized than he did of Rheims Cathedral where he was crowned king, saying: "For the dignity of a child of God which was bestowed on me in baptism is greater than that of the ruler of a kingdom. The latter I shall lose at death; the other will be my passport to everlasting glory."

Everything one does (in the state of grace) out of love for God and neighbor is meritorious. Every sacrament worthily received increases grace in the soul of the recipient (Council of Trent). Grace is, our Lord says, a fountain: "The water I give shall become a fountain within him, leaping up to provide eternal life" (Jn. 4:14). St. Mary Magdalene of Pazzi says that if a man in the state of sanctifying grace knew how pleasing his soul is to God, he would die of excess of joy.

The family of _____ must find comfort in the knowledge that he (she) did his (her) very best to keep God's laws, and live an exemplary Catholic life. It is because of this that those who suffer the pain of loss of a loved one can find solace in the words of St. John: "We are God's children now; what we shall later be has not yet come to light; we know that when it comes to light, we shall be like him [God], for we shall see him as he is" (1 Jn. 3:2).

The doctrine of the direct vision of God in heaven by the saved is a defined teaching (Council of Florence, 1439). The supernatural happiness of heaven consists in the intuitive vision of the Divine Essence. To enable the soul of a saved person to see and savor the great glory of God in heaven, it is supernaturally perfected by the *light of glory* (Council of Vienne, 1311). Oh, the wonder and the glory of it all!

Conclusion

Out of love, God sent His Divine Son to assume our human nature from the Virgin Mary. In becoming Man, Jesus Christ remained what He was and became what He was not, yet each nature stays distinct and forever undivided. Out of love for man, Christ endured a cruel death on the cross by which He ransomed us from our sins, opened heaven for those who accepted Him; and by His rising from the dead, He earned for us the resurrection of our body on the last day (1 Cor. 15:21). "O death, where is your victory? O death, where is your sting?" (1 Cor. 15:55)

Fewer than two thousand years ago, the Virgin Mary uttered her "Fiat," and God's Divine Son became Man to suffer and die so that we could be with Him in heaven. At this Mass, and at every Mass, the priest will say over the bread: "This is my Body," and over the wine, "This is my Blood"; and Christ, the Savior of the world, will be present on the altar as He was on Calvary, interceding for the living and the dead.

Let us commend the gentle soul of _____ to His tender care!